LAWRENCIA'S
LAST
PARANG

LAWRENCIA'S LAST PARANG

A Memoir of Loss and Belonging

as a Black Woman in Canada

ANITA JACK-DAVIES

INANNA memoir series

www.inanna.ca
Toronto, Ontario, Canada

The publisher gratefully acknowledges the support of the Canada Council for the Arts and the Ontario Arts Council. The publisher is also grateful for the financial assistance received from the Government of Canada.

Cover design: Val Fullard

Library and Archives Canada Cataloguing in Publication

Title: Lawrencia's last parang : a memoir of loss and belonging as a Black woman in Canada / Anita Jack-Davies.
Names: Jack-Davies, Anita, author.
Series: Inanna memoir series.
Description: Series statement: Inanna memoir series | Includes bibliographical references.
Identifiers: Canadiana (print) 20230467415 | Canadiana (ebook) 20230467695 | ISBN 9781771338097 (softcover) | ISBN 9781771338103 (EPUB) | ISBN 9781771338110 (PDF)
Subjects: LCSH: Jack-Davies, Anita. | LCSH: Jack-Davies, Anita—Family. | LCSH: Canada—Race relations. | CSH: Black Canadians—Race identity. | CSH: Trinidadian Canadians—Race identity. | CSH: Black Canadian women—Biography. | CSH: Black Canadians—Biography. | CSH: Trinidadian Canadians—Biography. | LCGFT: Autobiographies.
Classification: LCC FC106.B6 Z7 2023 | DDC 305.48/896071092—dc23

Printed and bound in Canada

Inanna Publications and Education Inc.
210 Founders College, York University
4700 Keele Street, Toronto, Ontario M3J 1P3 Canada
Telephone: (416) 736-5356   Fax: (416) 736-5765
Email: inanna.publications@inanna.ca Website: www.inanna.ca

This book is dedicated to my daughter Kennedy Lawrencia Elaine Davies. What did I do to deserve you, my Mami? There were moments when I was writing the book and you came over to console me. Yours is a kindness and sweetness that most mothers yearn for.

CONTENTS

Soundtrack to Lawrencia's Last Parang

Music has played an important role in the Jack family, now and ever since we've known ourselves. Writing this memoir would have been incomplete without the sounds of Trinidad and the Caribbean broadly speaking. I wanted to bring the reader into the culture of the island and of our home. My hope is that readers will use the YouTube playlist that accompanies each chapter to set the mood and tone for the words on the page. As a lover of music, the soundtrack to this memoir has been carefully curated to reflect specific places and times that are referenced in the text, as well as the music that my family actually played throughout the years.

Track I:
PARADISE LOST

Parang: the staged act of merrymaking, music, dance, and food typical of the Spanish Creole community of Trinidad. (Amelia Ingram, 2002)

<u>Soundtrack</u>:

Golpe
Daisy Voisin

Nosotros Tenemos
Daisy Voisin

Good Mother
Jann Arden

Doh Rock It So
Baron

One More Time
Machel Montano

Fire and Rain
James Taylor

I Shot the Sheriff
Bob Marley

Blueberry Hill
Fats Domino

O N DECEMBER 6, 2013, I was awakened from deep sleep by a telephone call from my cousin in Boston.

It was 6:00 a.m. I opened my eyes just enough to find the cordless phone on my bedside table. It was Christmas time and we were living in a large house on a country road in Kingston, Ontario, Canada. The table was crowded with lotion, *InStyle* magazines, a nail clipper, Beats headphones, a water bottle and my Bible. I grabbed the phone on the first ring to avoid waking Kennedy who slept in her bedroom down the hallway, near the guest bedroom, but the network of telephones dispersed in rooms throughout the house announced the caller and made a loud echo that bounced through the foyer's chandelier.

On the other end of the line she delivered the news. "I'm calling you to tell you that Mami died last night." Unsure about whether I was dreaming, I searched for words. "No, I spoke with Mami last night and she sounded good...she's good." "No, she died last night," Stacey insisted with an urgency in her voice that registered the certainty of her words. She needed me to hear the truth rather than the fiction that I wanted to believe. Stunned and unable to process what I heard, I was flushed by a feeling of dread. In an instant, I was forced to come to terms with the passing of the mother who raised me even though my biological mother was still alive.

After returning the phone to the emptiness of its base, I relayed the news to my husband. "Mami died last night..." And then I began to wail. I've never heard myself cry like that before. The deep bellowing moan escaping my body signalled to the universe that my veil of protection was torn. It was a veil of protection that only became apparent to me once she had passed. Her love was the armour that shielded me throughout my life. I felt alone and afraid, even though Daddy was still alive. I knew that there was still deep snow on the ground outside and the news of her passing made me feel as though someone had stripped me naked and left me to stand alone in the freezing cold. I asked myself how I could live without a mother, especially with Kennedy being so young.

To console myself somewhat, I thought about how all of Mami's children were healthy: Aunty Marian, Aunty Juliet, Aunty Gemma, Aunty Erroline, Uncle Joseph, Aunty Linda, Aunty Joslin, and Aunty Germine. Minutes later when the sobbing stopped, I reminded myself that I had to be strong for Kennedy, but my body was lifeless. I felt exhausted. There was an emptiness inside my chest, near my heart, a sensation that I had never felt before. I am not sure whether I imagined the pain or whether it was really there. Laying on the bed and looking up at the light fixture in the middle of the ceiling, I recall watching its pewter arms holding six white cups illuminated by its light. My mind was racing. The walls of our bedroom were a green-grey colour. It reminded me of the cement that Daddy mixed in the yard on Saturday mornings when I was six years old. I remember the shade because I had asked the designer from Reid and Siemonsen to help me pick colours for the room that would remind me of being at the spa. I didn't know then how much I would rely on my bedroom, and the adjacent room that we turned into my closet, for refuge.

On the opposite side of the bedroom was a ginormous bookshelf that filled the length of the wall. It was meticulously adorned with books, encyclopedias, pictures of Kennedy in silver frames, vases with flowers, and an assortment of knick-knacks that we collected over the course of our marriage. The silk curtains that hugged the only window in the room were to my left and parted slightly, which allowed for the dawn light to seep in.

When Kennedy awoke, we sat her between us on our bed. Taking turns, we explained Mami's passing in the way that adults speak to children about things too difficult for their comprehension. We told her that I would be leaving Kingston in a few days to attend the funeral in Trinidad. At five years old, she looked at me with a mixture of confusion and fear and began to cry. I could not tell if she cried because she knew that I was upset or if she truly remembered who Mami was. Kennedy was only a year old when we took her to Trinidad for the first time in 2009. After returning to Canada, she spoke to Mami and Daddy whenever I called home. I often gave her the phone to say "Hello" towards the end of my conversations. I coached her to tell Mami, "I love you," and "I miss you," and Mami would reply in her melodious Trini song, "Yes, Doodo, and I love you too." I was relieved that we visited Trinidad when Mami was still alive. I didn't know then that she would be snatched from my life so soon. We hadn't gone on enough mother-daughter dates. I hadn't asked her all the questions that I needed to ask. She didn't hear about my consulting business or about Kennedy attending a French school.

I thought I had more time. Later that day, I milled about the house with Kennedy and made plans for the funeral. I kept the television on in the kitchen and relied on the news coverage to keep my mind occupied on something other than Mami's passing. The death of Nelson Mandela was on heavy rotation on CNN. Barack Obama was in his second term as president of the United States and had recently delivered a speech on income inequality, which was being critiqued by media pundits across multiple news outlets.

That was well before the coronavirus pandemic of 2020. Well before the entire globe experienced unprecedented loss and grief. Well before COVID-19 and sheltering in place invaded our lives and forced a vigilance around health and safety protocols the world has never seen. I didn't know then that loss would have taken root, seeking shelter in our bones, our brains, and our genitals, sending millions to an early grave. In Canada, we lost 51,921 lives (Government of Canada, 2023), but the global number was 6.9 million (World Health Organization, 2023). I couldn't have predicted such anguish and am relieved that Mami did not have to live through it. The news of her death felt like the wretched prank of a pimple-faced teenager on a muggy summer night. I couldn't think about my future then, paralyzed as I was. But it was the finality of it all that left me feeling desperate.

LAWRENCIA "SHOON" JACK (née Garcia) was born in Trinidad on November 14, 1934 in Guaracara village between Mayo and Tabaquite. Named after her favourite uncle Shonito, her father, Benacio "Papa" Garcia, was born in Venezuela and lived in Moruga his entire life. Her mother, Virginia "Mama" Garcia, was Black and born in Trinidad. She was the second oldest of nine siblings: Lena, Reynold, Juanita, Louisa, Geraldo, Daniel, Frederick, Martha, and Stephanie. Mami and Daddy married on May 14, 1954 in a small ceremony at the Warden's Office in San Fernando. Mami called herself "Cocoa Panyol." Unique to Trinidad and Tobago, Cocoa Panyols describe the Spanish speaking peoples of Trinidad. Historically, they were migrant workers from Venezuela who worked the cocoa plantations between the nineteenth century and first half of the twentieth century (Moodie-Kablalsingh, 1992). The term literally brings together the "cocoa" of the agricultural product itself with "Panyol," which was meant to denote "Español" or Spanish speaking. With their arrival on the island, the workers also brought with them a tradition of playing "La Parranda" or parang, a Christmas tradition of carolling and merrymaking with the distinct sounds of the cuatro, the maracas, and the mandolin, key instruments of the modern day parang band.

Papa and Mama were good people. Papa worked the garden and Mama was a homemaker. I don't know whether Papa ever worked a regular job as we know it. He was much shorter than Mama with sombre eyes and a quiet demeanour. They both had large tattoos on their arms and I always wondered whether they were once rowdy teenagers who got them in acts of defiance or whether they got them as part of a trend that swept the island in their youth. They were kind to us as children. Papa and Mama lived in a small wooden house on what looked like an expansive estate in Guaracara. There was one main road leading to and from the village. When standing at the top of the hill near the path to the house, I could see what looked like a thick lush forest, peppered by small houses, some of which were made of brick. The road leading down the hill was narrow and bumpy and as children we bobbed up and down if we were sitting at the back of Daddy's Mitsubishi truck on the way there.

Papa and Mama used an oil lamp and had no electricity or running water. They lived off the land. Whenever we visited, Papa made us coffee in an old black pot that he had since his youth. I bet a pot like that would sell for hundreds of dollars today on eBay. The coffee was from the cocoa estate nearby or at least that's how I understood it as a child. Papa had a special way of making it that I didn't quite understand. He was often hunched over a fire in preparation and served it to us in white enamel cups. Its flavour was sweet, bitter, and creamy all at the same time. To this day, I have yet to taste anything that matches it. Whenever we visited, we played around the house and ran down the hill. We ate Governor's plums and looked for mangoes or cherries on trees that we found on the land.

Mami was Papa's favourite. That is the truth. Daddy told me this in confidence one day while we were on the veranda. Mami was busy talking to Aunty Juanita in the kitchen, which was located at the back of the house, and could not hear him. I often wondered about her being the favourite and whether that made her brothers and sisters angry, jealous, or resentful of her. I remember the way Papa looked at her, his eyes laden with love and admiration and how fond she was of him. As children, we knew that there was juicy gossip about Mami's siblings, but most of it was hidden from us. Daddy didn't elaborate. He delivered the news and quickly changed the topic, leaving me frantic for more. Based on what I saw, Mami was the most successful of all of her siblings. She lived in the nicest house and had lovely clothing, jewellery, and a nice car. She and Daddy sent my Uncle Joseph to study law at Cambridge University in the UK, based on funds Daddy saved from his job at Trinidad Cement Limited in Claxton Bay. Daddy afforded Mami a privileged lifestyle, even with their humble beginnings.

Sometimes Papa walked for forty-five minutes from Guaracara to our home to be with her. I remember when I was about six years old and Papa came to our home unexpectedly. He wore an old white t-shirt that turned grey from years of use, dark cotton trousers, and flip-flops that had sunken to the shape of his feet, showing his peach-coloured toes in the sweltering heat. Mami brought him into the house, sat him on the couch, and fed him cow heel soup to sober him up. He had had too much to drink and Mami was visibly annoyed. Papa's drinking was something that we had gotten used to, but we never used terms such as "alcoholic," even if his drinking got out of hand. He said out loud that Mami was his favourite, his eyes roaming the expanse of the living room. His sentences were a mixture of gibberish and knowledge, with sprinkles of wisdom thrown into the melee. Mami was abrupt. She told him to hush and to stop speaking nonsense, but I knew that he was telling the truth.

As a teenager Mami left Guaracara and worked as a live-in nanny near Whiteland. It was here that she and Daddy first met. Patrick Joseph Jack was born on January 12, 1932. He was the first of seven children, including Virginia, Veronica, Eva, Gwendolyn, Raphael, and Wendy. His mother, Grandma Hessie Charles, was born in Trinidad, but his father, Edwards Richards, a bass player in a local band, was born in Grenada. Daddy attended Eccles Village primary school in Whiteland and fell in love with Mami while singing at church in Mayo. Daddy recalled that when he first laid eyes on her, he thought she was the most beautiful girl in the village. Sitting on our front porch, Daddy described her skin, a smooth café mocha, her hazel eyes, and long wavy hair. I could sense that Daddy was proud that he was able to marry a woman like Mami, especially since she was Panyol and he was Black. He didn't quite put it that way, but during another one of our chats he explained that friends and family members were surprised that Mami chose him because he was dark-skinned and clearly not what he described as Spanish. I often wondered whether Daddy learned to sing parang as well as he did in order to become an honorary Panyol. And I recognized the look in his eyes when he spoke about being dark-skinned. It was a look that told me that there was much more pain beneath the surface. Being dark-skinned myself, I bonded deeply with him at that moment.

When Daddy sang parang, if I closed my eyes, I could have sworn that I was listening to a Venezuelan. Over the years, Papa taught Daddy the parang standards: "Sereno Sereno," "Hurrah Hurrah," and "De Verdad." Before long, Daddy was playing parang with Papa and other men from villages close by. When Daddy sang with his raspy tenor voice, he was the most handsome man in the world to me. And in his retelling about how he met Mami, Daddy said that he admired her figure and that she was "...big like a barrel." Mami overheard him and began to quarrel. Smiling, Daddy spoke in a softer tone as he shared about their early life together in Whiteland. Daddy recalled that what he most admired about Mami was her voice, which he described as a bell. As children, parang and live music was simply a part of life. We were encouraged to sing, dance, and express ourselves musically. We watched Mami and Daddy interact with friends and family during the parang season and it was their shared love of music that created the foundation for their lives and for our family. They didn't know it at the time, but through this gift of music, Mami and Daddy gave us something that we are now passing on to our children and for that, I remain indebted.

Early in their marriage, Daddy worked as a tile maker at Huggins in San Fernando, even though he trained as a carpenter. Daddy always spoke fondly of his early days in the trade. After leaving Huggins, he was hired as a foreman at Trinidad Cement Limited. I still see the vision in my mind's eye of the day he was honoured with an award at work. Daddy brought the newspaper clipping home and stuck it on the corner of this headboard, in the inner box where the wood and glass met. In the photo, he shook hands with a man wearing a suit. I remember how strange it felt seeing him in the picture, beaming with pride. It was the first time that I saw Daddy as someone other than my father. I saw that he had a life outside our home. He was good at his craft and not simply the patriarch of our family.

Daddy and Mami moved to Whiteland and began clearing the land to build the house that I lived in as a child. That house was wooden and stood on high stilts that allowed us to play on the dirt floor underneath. There was a long drawing room and three adjacent bedrooms. A steep staircase led to the front of the house and a back staircase was used to access the kitchen, which stood on the far end of the home. Beside the house was a large mango tree. When the ripe mangoes fell to the soft earth below, we sprinted down the stairs, almost risking our lives to be the first to score the juicy treat. The most important feature of that house though was the large veranda: it enabled us to see passersby who often called out to us with a good morning cheer, or friends and relatives who honked their horns as they whizzed by on Poonah Road. Today we call it the "old house" since a newly constructed home sits near this plot of land today. Beyond their nine children, Mami and Daddy had twenty-two grandchildren and fifteen great-grandchildren at the time of her passing, most of whom live in Boston, New York, Canada, and England.

We called Lawrencia "Mami." In my family, and in Caribbean culture broadly speaking, the term "Mami" is a term of endearment and can refer to women and girls. I call Kennedy "Mami" now. My birth certificate, issued by the Office of the Registrar General for the City of Toronto, recorded my name as Anita Patricia Jack. The certificate says that my biological mother resided at a home for girls. She had me as a teenager, but was unable to care for me and Mami and Daddy stepped in. They told her that they would take over my care and alleviate the stress of being a new mother in a new country.

THE MAP OF TRINIDAD tells me that the place where I grew up does not exist even though it is the only place that Mami ever lived. Poonah Road, Whiteland, is located in the south of the island and I can see the place with my eyes closed. Its landscape has become etched into my brain after all these years. Named for the white sand that ran through our fingers as children, Poonah Road is one major throughway that locals use to travel from San Fernando to Couva, Tabaquite, Piparo to the north or Princes Town and St. Madeleine to the south. My aunts and uncle attended elementary school in Mayo, and each year the village hosts a large soca bazaar that attracts music fans from all corners of the island.

I cannot remember when I first arrived in Whiteland. The thick forest that meets us each day from the front porch seems to have always been a part of me. Delicate hibiscus flowers and an assortment of plants can be found everywhere: the red anthurium, stinging nettles, the pink and green caladium, and the poinsettia. Mami was an avid gardener and tended to her garden, often to the point of illness. Birds, grasshoppers, roaches with wings, spiders, frogs, worms, and lizards remain vividly clear. As children we played as chickens, ducks, and stray dogs milled about the yard. We sometimes saw snakes, some large, some small, but always colourful, sliding through the bush. At one point, Daddy kept pigs. Our pigpen stank and was a horrendous sight. I recall the smell of a disinfectant he used to mask the stench. Daddy threw it on the muck-filled floor and scrubbed the muddy poop from the concrete with large buckets of water. Using a wooden broom with stiff bristles, he whistled while he worked, wearing gloves, shorts that were cut unevenly, and rubber boots with no laces. I loved being outside and loved exploring the different parts of the yard.

One day, while playing with my cousins, Mami picked up a white chicken that roamed the yard and with three swift yanks, broke its neck. I watched in awe as she ignored the chicken's cries. An hour later, we ate it, savouring the stew that she mastered and had become known for. I wondered how Mami, so delicate and ladylike, could be so brave, so vicious. I was not fond of animals and the thought of touching the chicken made my skin crawl. Once, Daddy had company over, mostly men, and they killed a pig from the pen. I will never forget the sound the pig made as it took its last breath. It was the frantic and hysterical squeal of an animal who knew its end was near. The sound was chillingly haunting and even though I was nowhere near where the men were as they made the kill, my entire body was stricken with fear. These were my first experiences with death and dying.

F ROM OUR FRONT PORCH drivers sped by on Poonah Road. Now and again, Mami left her cooking in the kitchen to see if we needed snacks: penny cool, tolumb, sugar cake, tamarind balls, curried mangoes, sweet mangoes, kurma, doubles, or pholourie. As the drivers went about their haste, one could hear the sound of soca music blaring from the loud speakers, paying homage to the year's Road March. The road is where the excitement lived.

Daddy often sat on the veranda at different points throughout the day. Neighbours called out to him as they walked by on the main road, each expecting him to be in the same spot on the brown leather recliner. Mami took care of Daddy. She brought him meals, told him when it was time to nap, and filled him in on the gossip of the day. She was his eyes and his ears. Mami and Daddy were friends. They were best friends and they had a tenderness for each other that I admired. In all my life, I never heard Daddy raise his voice at Mami, even though there were times when he looked visibly angry at her. He treated her with gentleness and respected her. He never cut her off while she spoke and never spoke over her. He was always a gentleman, even at the very end.

Track 2:
WHERE'S THE PROFESSOR?

Soundtrack:

Midnight in Harlem
Tedeschi Trucks Band

Into the Mystic
Van Morrison

Gravity
John Mayer

Jireh
Elevation Worship & Maverick City

Sending Me Angels
Delbert McClinton

Dream a Little Dream of Me
Ella Fitzgerald & Louis Armstrong

Have You Ever Seen the Rain
Creedence Clearwater Revival

Road to Zion
Damian Marley ft. Nas

WHEN MAMI DIED, I was teaching the course *IDIS 302: Race and Racism* in the Department of Geography at Queen's University. I was already feeling unhappy and out of place at the university and the news of Mami's passing made me feel like giving up on teaching altogether. I didn't want to be there anymore. Mami's death forced me to come to terms with the turmoil that I was feeling about my career. I had been procrastinating about it for a while, but her passing forced me to face the inevitable. My students were preparing to submit their final essays. It was my second time teaching a part-time course at Queen's University. I took it on with the hopes of landing a full-time academic position. I thought that teaching part-time would help me land a position as a "real professor," but the very nature of such itinerant work almost guaranteed my career's demise. But no one ever told me that. I knew deep down inside that I needed to make a decision about whether I would continue applying for academic roles at a time when few universities were hiring.

Please remember though that the culture of the academy is toxic. It is an unhealthy place. I found the academy to be cutthroat, disingenuous, and racist. At the time, I had only worked and studied at Queen's and to be fair, I had nothing else to compare it to. Daddy once shared that he saw me teaching in a large lecture hall one day. I didn't have the heart to tell him the truth about my unhappiness with the academy. In 2011 when I graduated from my doctoral program, I knew that moving to another city to pursue academic work was out of the question given that I was a new mother. And while "adjuncting" allowed me to interact with students, being a "sometimes professor" was a far cry from the vision I had for myself when I entered the doctoral program.

When I applied to the doctoral program, I wanted to teach at the university in the hopes of making a difference. I knew that there were few Black academics and knew that my presence at the front of the classroom would have an impact on students based on my lived experience and expertise. My advisers and mentors encouraged me to pursue academic work, especially since it would provide an avenue for me to write for a living. My main thesis supervisor in the doctoral program, Dr. Magda Lewis, pulled me aside and told me that my writing had promise. She explained that if I were to become a professor, I could actually make a living serving my gift. She pointed out that I already had teaching experience as an elementary school teacher and that a PhD would give me a breadth of understanding in the field of education that would be unrivalled. Dr. Lewis looked out for me. She guided me and showed me that it was possible for me to pursue academic work on a full time basis. Most importantly, I saw the professorship as a career that would provide me with the flexibility to be a mom to Kennedy. The professors I knew had flexibility with their schedules and I needed that flexibility because motherhood was quickly proving to be more difficult than I had originally anticipated.

As much as I struggled with my place in the academy, I realized that being there, even as a "sometimes professor" was still something. I was able to teach and to share my point of view which is a privileged position to be in. I decided the content of the syllabus…what to keep in, what to take out, what to focus on, what to ignore. This is what power looks like. With the start of each new course and with each new group of students, I worked hard to establish my authority and credibility. Compared with white professors, I did not assume that the title "professor," "instructor," or "PhD" had any meaning for my students because of my Black skin.

What I know for sure is that I was not afforded the same respect by students as white professors were and for me, the academy was never a place where I felt safe. Starting in grad school, my identity and my work on race or critical theory was met with suspicion and scorn. In grad school, my colleagues learned the rules: how to meet at each other's houses to learn about research projects, how to make friends with professors who assigned the A pluses needed for plumb grants, how to smile with one's mouth but never with one's eyes. The most important lesson that grad school taught me was to never trust a person in academia. There were so many instances where confidences were broken or when I thought that a colleague wanted to start a genuine friendship, only to realize that what they really wanted was "help" from me to start a diversity-related initiative. I was often completely overlooked or seen for what I could do for others.

Weeks into the semester when students turned in their midterm essays, one-quarter of them failed to include the PhD behind my name. Some addressed me as "Mrs." and "Ms." One wrote my name down as Jack (first name) and Davies (last name), period. Soon afterwards, I asked a white female colleague if she experienced these same slights. The professor looked at me with both concern and confusion by what she described as "disrespect." Because I was a sometimes professor, I worked in isolation from the collegiality that full-time professors enjoyed and there were few opportunities for me to discuss my experiences with students openly and honestly as a Black woman in that role.

My colleague shared that she did not experience such microaggressions. Reflecting upon her words, I couldn't figure out if the students' blatant disrespect for my title had to do with my race, my gender, or both. I felt awful. There is no rage like the fire that burns inside of you on account of being disrespected by a kid whose parents pay for everything. I suppose that some of my students experienced cognitive dissonance because I led the course. This dissonance is in response to my low status in Canadian society compared with the authority that the professorship commands. As leader of the course, I was able to assign a final grade for each student, a mark that determined whether they were accepted to law school, medical school, or any professional program of their choice. Students raised to believe that Black people are inferior to white people may resist my decision-making authority and this often plays out in complicated and disturbing ways that the academy ought to be paying better attention to, but won't.

But resistance to my authority and my Black skin was not simply restricted to students, but to administrative assistants, support-staff, caretakers, security guards, academic colleagues, deans, and senior administrators. My authority was challenged by two teaching assistants, a South Asian female and a Black male. It took the form of questioning decisions that I made, offering unsolicited "constructive criticism" about the course during meetings, enabling students to criticize my teaching during tutorials, and verbalizing disagreement over my decision to grant extensions when students wrote to me requesting them. I often wondered if they dared to challenge white professors in this way.

That semester I found myself questioning why I chose to enter this wretched profession in the first place and how much of the nonsense I was willing to put up with. With Mami's passing, I needed to put the academy in its rightful place in my life. I was unhappy and afraid to admit it. Something deep down told me that I was on the wrong path, yet I felt this tremendous pressure to stick with it. On some level, I didn't want to disappoint Mami and Daddy. I wanted them to be proud of me and I knew that they were. I found myself holding on to the academy because I did not have a backup plan or a way to transition to another line of work. I was unsure about my next steps and rather than making another mistake, I held on to teaching for dear life. I held on because letting go was much too scary for me to contemplate and the thought of Mami and Daddy being disappointed that I was no longer a professor was more than I could bear. Daddy in particular bragged and boasted about me to the point where it became part of his identity. His pride in me became a badge of honour that he held so dear and I couldn't bring myself to destroy that. The truth is that I couldn't bring myself to leave the academy at that time. Planning Mami's funeral provided just the distraction I needed.

I became interested in becoming a professor so that I could write books. I knew that writing was my gift. Because I was already a certified teacher, teaching at the university level did not phase me at all. It was the other aspects of the job that I really hated, like research. I did not like spending hours upon hours filling out research applications that seemed like make-work projects. There were so many aspects of the role that felt as though the rules were more complicated than they needed to be. It felt as though somewhere in the past, the powers that be decided that life in the academy had to be difficult, convoluted, and opaque, with few levels of accountability. And because the "rules" were never written down, I always felt as though my success was at the whim of a department head, dean, or others in positions of authority. When I realized that I could actually write without being tethered to it, this brought me calm and a sense of comfort that I needed, but I wasn't ready to walk away from the dream that I created about the academy.

ACADEMIA HAS A DISTINCT and unique culture. It is a culture that a newcomer must learn; however, no one shared the rules with me. How unfair. It was as though I was expected to run a race, without anyone identifying where the starting blocks were, which direction I was expected to run in, or whether I was expected to run a 100-metre dash or a relay. The rules of the academy remain hidden so that only a select few are allowed to enter and remain within it. That select few does not include individuals like me. And so, I entered academia unaware of its culture. I did not realize that my ignorance would cost me dearly. On numerous phone calls to Mami and Daddy I tried to describe the climate, but they did not understand. They had no frame of reference for what I was experiencing: how to choose a thesis supervisor, preparing for the comprehensive exam, my grad school colleagues vandalizing my work space, watching as my colleagues were invited to socials or events with professors and learning that I had been left out. At the time, I couldn't figure out if the exclusion that I experienced had to do with my race, gender, or both.

Academia is a culture of nods and smiles. It is a culture where decisions are made behind closed doors. It is a culture where your friends and enemies appear to be one and the same. Nothing is clear. Mami and Daddy helped me through the difficult times as best as they could.

They worried about me. They prayed for me and I held on to that. At one point during grad school, my hair began falling out. I wasn't sure if it had to do with postpartum shedding after having Kennedy. When I called home to speak with Mami and Daddy, they asked me whether I wanted to drop out of the program and I explained that I wanted to stick with it. Mami and Daddy told me that if I wanted to leave, they would understand. Each day I arrived at my desk in the grad lounge at 9:00 a.m. and left at 5:00 p.m. Our study area was located in the basement of the building, a large concrete monstrosity located on the west end of the Queen's campus that was architecturally designed in the style of brutalism with few windows. The lounge had no window and was littered with computer stations and uncomfortable chairs. Upon entering the space, there was a kitchen area to the left and a sitting area with softer couches to the right. My desk area was situated at the very back of the lounge and offered me the illusion of privacy since there were no dividers between the workstations. I approached my studies with dedication and determination and thought of it as my full-time job. I had few friends and was lonely. Towards the end of my studies in 2010, I tore images of Black models from fashion magazines who were photographed with their asses bare. I plastered the images around my desk for passersby to see, making the message for what they could do crystal clear.

Mami and Daddy said holy novenas for me as Catholic parents. They gave offerings to a church in San Fernando and reassured me that I would finish the program. They poured encouragement into my soul as they learned of the ostracism and rejection that I experienced almost daily. Although I was never physically alone, going through the doctoral program at Queen's University remains one of the most difficult periods of my life.

In 2007, when I started the program, most of my students were white women. There were a few South Asian students, fewer Asian students, and no Black ones. I found myself at the front of the classroom with no faces that looked like mine. I taught a course on social justice in the fall of that year and for many, it was their first encounter with issues of race. Many were angry. The content of the course forced them to question everything that they had been taught up until that point in their lives and I was the bearer of bad academic news. Many were from the Toronto area and came from wealthy families. I was told that one student's father was the head of the Royal Bank of Canada. Who knows? Most were planning on returning to their hometowns to teach after securing their degrees, but I was most definitely their first Black professor and I sensed their unease. I watched in amusement as they sat waiting for the "professor" to arrive, even though I stood at the front of the classroom, organizing my things and getting myself ready for the day's lesson. Some of their discomfort stemmed from my identity being far removed from the symbols that we assign to knowledge...Albert Einstein comes to mind. I am far removed from the body out of which knowledge is supposed to emerge, and that body is white and male.

The fact that Queen's is a predominantly white university made the distance between my personal and professional identities all the more stark. My body was read as *out of place* on the campus. This distance forced me to engage in a form of emotional labour in the classroom that I hadn't initially anticipated. I needed to be doubly prepared for each lesson, in addition to looking after the practical aspects of the course: creating lecture slides, preparing lecture notes, responding to emails, and so on. But it was the emotional preparation that was draining as I wondered what I might possibly face each time I entered what felt like a lion's den.

My teaching was impacted by conceptions of my Black body as deviant, criminal, uneducated, and impoverished. These ideas and images determine whether students believe that I have anything to offer them. What it means to be Black in Canadian society goes before me and informs classroom interactions well before I begin a lecture. This is the reason why I was rarely recognized as "the professor" on the first day of class. Black women in Canada aren't professors, or at least that was the mood that I was met with. Nannies, yes. Cleaners at the Hilton Holiday

Inn, yes. Salesclerks at Bed, Bath and Beyond, yes, but never professors. When I taught, I entered the lecture hall already implicated by negative images of Black people, Black women, and women in general. It was a burden that I hadn't given any prior thought to until I began to teach.

Images of the whore, the mammy, the jezebel, the sapphire, and the "single mother" battle for space beside me at the front of the classroom. These are the images that our culture has carefully constructed about me and invite me to believe about myself. When I reject them because they are not who I am, I am called uppity. I am encouraged to politely accept the invitation to my suffering and exclusion with a smile. It's the Canadian way. Trapped, I cannot dislodge myself from these phantoms that steal my identity, an identity theft of sorts. I forced myself to prove that I embodied none of these stereotypes and tried to focus instead on the mechanics of teaching.

I remember one day in particular as I stood before the classroom looking out at the group of students, thirty-five in all. We were in a small seminar room with concrete walls everywhere. The desks were situated in rows. In the classroom, bulletin boards reflected the many projects that students worked on in science, social studies and mathematics. My desk was located in the front left corner of the classroom right beside a large blackboard. A blonde young woman, "Becky," wore a plaid shirt and boat shoes, a graduate of an all-girls private school I am sure… Havergal, Branksome, or Bishop Strachan. She rolled her eyes when I spoke. I felt like slapping that smirk off her face, rude and disrespectful wretch! A brunette, "Haley," sat in the front row with her arms folded and quickly looked away when our eyes met. She was sure never to hold my gaze. A young white man, "Justin" stared at me as though he was plotting to do me harm. He always sat in the same spot each week, at the back of the room, towards the right, with eyes that were barely seen from the half-moon brim of his baseball cap. I couldn't make out what he was thinking, but I knew that he was not happy with what I was saying about racism in Canada.

As I thought about leaving Kingston for Trinidad, my heart was heavy. I did not want to be teaching given the news of Mami's passing. As the professor, I could not show any vulnerability. It wasn't safe for me to do so as a Black woman working in a predominantly white setting. I adopted a "stiff upper lip" mentality and told myself that Mami's passing was something that my students did not need to know, and so, I went to class and pretended as though nothing had happened. Looking back now, I see what a mistake that was. I made decisions at the time given the circumstance that I found myself in. I was a Black woman teaching a course on race and racism at a predominantly white university, with little pay and no job security. Although Mami's passing forced me to seriously consider my teaching in the academy, the doubts were already there, like the pus that forms on a wound, and after a while, the throbbing reminds us that its release is the only thing that will make us feel better. Her death brought my unhappiness with the academy into sharper focus.

In coming to terms with Mami's passing, I began to consider what being Black in that context meant for me and whether I was willing to pay the price for sticking with it. To be Black in academia is to exist while being deemed invisible. It is to physically possess vocal cords while being invited to be silent. As a Black woman, I am invited from the time of my birth to see myself through the eyes of those who despise me. This is what Patricia Williams (1991) tells us in her text, *The Alchemy of Race and Rights*. I am taught that I embody everything that is negative. I am unholy. I am without virtue. I am undeserving and unlovable. My Black body in the academy disrupts the status quo because that space was never designed with me in mind. It is a space that was never designed for me to exist within its walls, especially since my teaching was a critique that dealt with issues of power, feminist theory, critical race theory, and white supremacy.

Teaching in the academy always felt to me like I was bridging incongruent worlds. It is soaked with double marginality. I must always be two people at once, both insider and outsider. It's akin to being invited to an exclusive party in Toronto's Forest Hill area to work the door! I exist simultaneously on the inside and the outside. I stand in the foyer, taking coats and providing small chits to the guests in return. I am on the inside, away from the cold. From my insider's vantage point, I enjoy somewhat of a privileged perspective. I can see the festivities as they unfold. I can admire the home…the paintings, the crown moulding, the chandeliers and furniture passed down from generation to generation. However, I can't enjoy it. I understand the role that I was hired to play. The role that I am to play is defined by the owner of the home…the person who has the power to fire me or tell me to leave. I am on the inside, but I am not one of them. I am on the inside, but everyone knows that I do not belong. I am on the inside and if I socialize too much, and move too far from my place, I will be snatched into my lane, albeit with a red-lipsticked smile and a pat on my shoulder from hands weighed down by a Rolex and a sapphire solitaire.

On the other hand, I am on the outside. My presence as "worker" in the confines of the coat-check area freezes my identity into place, despite my yearning to be seen as much more than the "coat-check girl." I am inside the mansion, but outside the circle. I am inside the building, but outside the culture of influence. I have some proximity to power even though that power is often beyond my reach. And as much as I see myself as more than a worker, I cannot escape my identity in that place and time.

And so, I am treated accordingly by the guests as they arrive. With my gaze, I secretly mark how the proud and impeccably dressed treat me. They inspect my clothing with haughty and disapproving eyes, summing up my worth with sly, furtive glances. My stationing in the barricaded area of the foyer situates my body as Other, as surplus, as helper…maid, slave. Standing behind the table, I am geographically restricted to being the "hired help." Some guests sail past me with a refusal to acknowledge my presence, deliberately avoiding my eyes. They fear that looking at me will make them less white, and so I am ignored. Others revel in the metaphorical consumption of my body, surveying my Black skin, chocolate as it were, my every curve, and thinking of things that cannot be said. And while I am physically present at the soiree, I remain in a conundrum. I am both welcomed and despised.

A S A BLACK WOMAN PROFESSOR, the space that I occupy at the front of the classroom is a negotiated one. It is not a given. I learned this at different points during my course when it was clear to me that the title "professor" carried a different meaning for me. The negotiation process takes place before, during, and after each course in ways that white professors do not have to think about, or at least not in the same way. My reputation, online presence, and interactions with students outside the classroom play a role in this process as well. I often walked into lectures unsure about whether I would experience racism or racial microaggressions that day.

In preparing to teach I was always conscious that I needed to take attention *away* from my body when I stood before my students. I worked to make my body *unknown* and irrelevant in light of the attention that my Black body attracts, whether I welcome this attention or not. I engaged in this emotional labour in an effort to earn my students' respect. I wanted them to listen to the ideas that I shared and had to work harder than my white colleagues to be seen as an academic. Where the white male academic is deemed a thinker, I am considered a single mother. Where the white male academic is deemed a researcher, I am considered a jezebel. Where the white male academic is deemed an intellectual, I am considered the help, emotional, and most importantly, angry and hysterical. More than anything else in this world, I am considered angry.

As a Black professor, I cannot escape my body because I am my body. I cannot dislodge myself from it. My body defines me. Because I am my body, I cannot deny its existence. I must respect the ways my body also becomes part of my pedagogy. I must reject the cultural invitation to regard my body as inferior to my mind because it informs my ability to belong to a place that sees my body as excess, as surplus. Week after week I agonized over what to wear for fear of appearing "too sexy." I could not run the risk of looking sexy at the front of the classroom. I got ready for work in my closet. It was my sanctuary, my go-to place if ever I felt sad or needed to think. A former bedroom, we turned it into a traditional dressing room, complete with four tall clothing racks and a chest of drawers that held my undies, scarves, and clothing too difficult to store on hangers. We had shelving put in by a local carpenter to hold my shoes and purses. On the floor was a large wooden chest that I used to store my workout clothing. Kennedy often joined me while I was getting ready. She played dress up, wearing my high-heeled shoes and trying on my hats. At times she climbed the shoe rack, looking to find treasure that may have been hidden from her view down below.

While getting ready for class, I fretted over one blouse after the next. Seeing my reflection in the heavy mirror that almost reached the ceiling, I threw unsuitable choices onto the mahogany Louis XIV chair or hastily returned them to their hangers because some were too revealing or tight around my breasts. One Tuesday evening, after frantically putting together one bad outfit after the next, I became hot and sweaty, even after my shower, and finally decided on wearing my favourite black trousers...only to notice my bum protruding from the corner of the mirror. With an exasperated sigh, I pulled out my go-to outfit: a black, long-sleeved dress. It was flattering but conservative. Time was running out and I couldn't be late for class.

Unlike my body, the white, male body disappears in the classroom. It is erased from the teaching process. His sometimes dishevelled clothing, uncombed hair, and unshaven face are accepted as normal because he is *not* of his body, but of his mind. Chacon (2006) speaks of this in her essay entitled, "Making Space for Those Unruly Women of Color." This Cartesian mind/body split positions the mind and the body on opposite sides of the spectrum. If the white male is of the mind, his role in the academy is to impart knowledge. His body is then suspended from reality. On the other hand, as a Black woman, my body is marked as unprofessional or less intelligent. My body is surveyed at all times and becomes hyper-visible. And this hyper-visibility is what I became most conscious of. The white male body is read as a geographical site of knowing, theory, teaching, and research in the academy. His attention to his mind, as opposed to his body, is not only a sign of his intellect, but also a sign of his whiteness. Whiteness carries meaning precisely because it is not reduced to the body in the same manner my body is.

During the course of race and racism, I walked a tightrope between being "nice" and being firm. The lecture hall was littered with students, sixty in total, with chairs erected in traditional lecture format. During class, two white male students sat near the front, staring at me, laughing and whispering in each other's ear. They did this in plain view for what felt like an eternity. I wanted to interrupt the lecture to tell them that they were being rude, but I didn't. I didn't want to appear angry even though I was offended. I stared back at them and moved closer to where they sat, hoping that my physical body would force the silence that I was looking for. The student who sat nearest to the aisle was closest to where I was standing. "Lennie" had vivid green eyes and the countenance of a used car salesman. His friend, whose name may have been "Curly," had dark brown hair and wore a navy blue hoodie with the Queen's logo on the front. When they noticed by my stare that I was not playing they stopped. After class, a bubbly white female bounced toward me in white Converse sneakers. She told me that she really enjoyed my classes and reassured me in a way I needed at that time. After most classes, as I gathered my things and unhooked my laptop from the AV system, a few male students passed by my desk as I shoved my papers and pencil case in my leather bag. They made eye contact with me, smiled, and told me that I did a great job.

Compared with me, the white male professor's intelligence renders his body *unseen*. Because my body is seen, my intelligence becomes unrecognizable. Students can deny his corporeality because his intelligence becomes a fact of his whiteness. Put another way, whiteness equals intelligence. I am not afforded this privilege. My body, already marred by codes of racial dysfunction, cannot escape the dominant gaze. What a difficult position for me to be in as an instructor at Queen's, regarded as one of Canada's most elite institutions and a university that has spoken of its dealing with racial insensitivity on the part of its student body on numerous occasions. I am thinking back to a Halloween party in 2005 when a white student dressed up as Miss Ethiopia and painted her face Black. A master's student at the time, I wrote an open letter to the Society of Graduate and Professional Students expressing my outrage, only to receive comments about the student's "innocence" and her lack of malicious intent in return. I wondered how Mami and Daddy could ever understand what it was like for me teaching at the university at that time. To some extent, I was actually relieved that they never experienced racism at the hands of white people throughout their lives. What I am certain about, however, is that there is nothing fragile about whiteness.

So while the white male professor's body is foreshadowed by his mind, my mind is foreshadowed by my body. This distinction is critical because it speaks to the work that I was forced to do in order to minimize my body each time I taught. His whiteness, and the fact that he has been authorized by the university to teach, makes sense to students. On the other hand, my body suggests that I have no place in the academy, and am certainly not in a position to impact their careers. Being reduced to my body is problematic because the academy is the business of the mind. The academy always has, and always will be, a preoccupation of the mind. And as a sometimes professor, I had to make the mind my top priority in order to survive.

Thinking back, I remember the horrendous course evaluation I received for the course on social justice in 2007. I was not entirely surprised by the comments, but they hurt. I questioned whether I should continue teaching at that time as they were often personal. One student advised me to "smile" more. Another criticized me for focusing on issues of race, as if to alert the university's administration that my teaching was "biased." I feared that low course evaluations would hinder my progress in the academy. Students often came to class unprepared to discuss issues of race and were unaware of Canada's problematic relationship with race. It became clear to me that their discomfort with me, and with my teaching, had so much to do with their prior knowledge. Readings and course materials that challenged them to consider their work with racialized and immigrant students were often seen as threatening, despite the fact we cannot teach without considering these issues. Yet, there was no institutional recognition that my teaching from a Black feminist perspective was different from teaching math and science. There continues to be a deafening silence surrounding this in the academy. My University Survey of Student Assessment of Teaching (USAT) evaluations provided the university with a supposed "objective" account of the students' opinions, but that assessment tool could never capture the extent to which students unleashed their anger and rage toward me and other racialized professors. Again, as Black people, we are rarely asked about our opinions and experiences.

When the university is read as a marketplace, students expect to receive a product or service in exchange for the fees that they pay. Thinking of education as a service, many do not expect to encounter a professor like me. Using the consumer model of education, my teaching can be read by students as having received the "wrong" product. Because they have received the wrong product, they expect a refund or an exchange of some sort. When neither of these options are available to them (too late to drop my course, no other courses available to switch into), course evaluations provide students with an outlet for that which cannot be said. Living in a culture that already despises women, and Black women in particular, students can register their displeasure with "the course."

Using this customer service model, the USAT becomes a pseudo client satisfaction survey that the university can rely on to improve their "products." Students come to understand that the evaluation will provide an opportunity for them to share opinions about an instructor or course that introduces them to new and uncomfortable material. The operative word here is "uncomfortable." Education should no longer move students out of their comfort zones or professors like me stand to pay a price. Using this customer service model, the uncomfortable material that I teach becomes nothing more than a defective product. Rather than think about new and difficult knowledge as *needed* in order to effectively teach students from diverse backgrounds, many considered this knowledge inherently faulty, political, and *out of place* in the field of education.

I remember a lecture where I had invited "Kyle," a white, male, school teacher from the Kingston area to do a guest lecture in my course. I asked him to discuss his approaches to critical pedagogy at the high school level. We were colleagues in graduate school and he was committed to a teaching practice that challenged assumptions about race, gender, social class, and so on. During the lecture, he spoke passionately about his teaching and about the risks involved in challenging the status quo. His teaching strategies adhered to key principles that I hoped for my students to learn. After class, I was surprised to see how quickly white female students formed a long line in order to speak to him. These were the same students who had rarely uttered a word in my class and simply left my classroom after each lecture ended. With twinkling eyes and a twirl of their hair, they stood before him wanting to "know" more.

I walked away asking myself why my students responded so positively to him, when, in essence, we discussed the same teaching strategies. Why were his words so well received? Their response to white male authority was dumbfounding to me. The USATs and other teaching evaluation tools are ineffective and unfair in measuring teaching that is *designed* to disrupt their taken-for-granted views. Such tools fail to capture that student assessment of my teaching reflects nothing more than who *they* are, *their* wants and *their* needs.

As a sometimes professor in the university classroom I am vulnerable. One misunderstood incident is enough to cast suspicion and doubt about me and my job. Each time I teach about race, I must come to terms with the risks that I take when I enter the lecture hall. I wonder for a moment if I might get insurance coverage for it. I wonder if a company like Liberty Mutual or GEICO would take me on as a client. The insurance policy would have to cover the scorn, ridicule, microaggressions, and microinsults that Black professors often face when we dare to teach in spaces that were never intended for us. I wonder what the insurance agent might say upon hearing my voice, "I beg your pardon Dr. Jack-Davies, you would like to be insured for what?"

Near the end of my doctoral program in 2011, I called home to speak with Mami and Daddy to talk about work. I told them that I was thinking about starting a diversity consulting business because I could see the dead-end that being a sometimes professor was. He and Mami took turns asking me questions. They asked me whether the pay would be guaranteed and when I said no, Daddy wanted to know if my husband Eric had given me permission. I said yes. After listening intently, as was his way, he probed with a few more inquiries about travelling away from Kingston and about Kennedy being so young. Mami also suggested that I shouldn't do anything that would make Eric angry. Before ending the conversation, Daddy told me that it was not such a good idea for me to leave teaching and that I should stick to it some more because teaching was what I was born to do. Disappointed, I hung up the phone. While occupied with Mami and Daddy on the phone, I found Kennedy in my ensuite washroom. She had gotten into my makeup bag and the lipstick was everywhere: on her face, her teeth, scrunched between her hands, smudged on the wooden cabinets and the concrete floor. And as I tidied the mess with Windex and paper towels, I thought about their advice and wondered what to do about the fact that I did not intend to take it.

Track 3:
DANTE'S INFERNO

<u>Soundtrack</u>:

Hurrah, Hurrah
Daisy Voisin

El Diablo Suerte
Daisy Voisin

Dreamlover
Mariah Carey

Lion's Paw
Tarrus Riley

Unconditional Love
Jah Cure

Kingly Character
Garnett Silk

We Sound
Xtatic

Into the Mystic
Van Morrison

Wotless
Kes the Band

I'm on Fire
Bruce Springsteen

CHRISTMAS IS A BITTERSWEET time of year for the Jack family. During my first year of studies at the University of Toronto, our house burned to the ground, leaving Mami and Daddy with the shirts on their backs, weeks before Christmas Day. The phone rang. It was a long-distance call from Trinidad. I heard Aunty Juliet's voice on the other end of the line. I was working part-time at the "Tickets N Tobacco" kiosk at Sears in Toronto's Woodbine Centre. The new concession stands were somewhat of a novelty in Canada. They offered smokers the ability to purchase their fixes while shopping for Maytag refrigerators. My aunt's voice was measured and sure. I remember that it rained terribly that day. Through the skylight directly above the cash register, the raindrops were ferocious and competed for my attention. Aunty Juliet reassured me that no one was hurt in the fire, but we lost everything. Tears filled my eyes, but I pretended I was not crying. I tried to be strong for her. My knees were weak and I was afraid. A thousand thoughts raced through my mind as I listened: What will happen to Mami and Daddy... where will they live...do we have insurance?

The fire was a devastating blow they never got over. How could they? Daddy built that house with his own hands. Some say that he was never the same. Years later, he and Mami spoke of the fire as though it had happened only days before. A spark from the electrical pole that stood near Poonah Road, the main road that connects Bonne Aventure and Whiteland, was responsible for the blaze. Daddy recalled how the spark travelled down the wire that led to the gas tank in our kitchen. The tank provided gas to our stove. I can't remember now if the stove was painted blue or whether Mami purchased it that way from Standard Furniture in San Fernando. In an instant, he and Mami watched as the flames ravaged everything that they worked a lifetime to build.

At the time of the fire, Mami was next door at Aunty Marian's house, a one-family home that was built on the same lot when I was a child.

I lived with Mami and Daddy as a toddler; however, once I started attending school, I lived with Aunty Marian, Uncle Reagy, and their two daughters. Although I slept with Aunty Marian's family, I went back and forth between the two households seamlessly, given how close the homes were in proximity to each other. I saw Mami each and every day. My living with Aunty Marian was to ease the burden on Mami in terms of combing my hair and getting me ready for school. In this way, Aunty Marian became a mother to me and Uncle Reagy a father. They helped out with my care and shouldered the day-to-day responsibilities. Throughout my life, my aunts and uncle cared for me in different ways because everyone understood that my biological mother lived in Canada.

Daddy was tending to his chickens and ducks in the yard, as he did on weekends or after driving his Maxi Taxi to earn extra money on the side. He couldn't even save the seven macaws who scorched to death in their cages on the front porch, the black smoke engulfing their cries. The cages hung from enormous silver hooks that were bolted to the wood joists. Each morning one of the birds sang, "Patrick wants a cracker!" upon seeing him. To this greeting, Daddy responded with a clucking noise from his throat, a sound that reminded me of gargling Listerine, and provided their sustenance for the day. Years later, Daddy recounted that the fire made the TV6TNT Six O'Clock news. As he spoke, I noticed a sadness in his ash-coloured eyes that I had never noticed before. And because I couldn't bear to see him cry, I quickly changed the topic and asked him if he and Mami got any parang lately.

On one trip home in my early twenties, I borrowed a clothing iron from Mami. It was 5:00 a.m. and we were getting ready to go to market in Marabella, a small town nestled between San Fernando to the south and Pointe-a-Pierre to the north. The bungalow was dark and silent. Daddy lay asleep in his room, which was located at the southernmost part of the house. From his room, there was a door that led to Aunty Juanita's room. Aunty Juanita is Mami's younger sister and often visited from Guaracara, where Papa lived, to lend a helping hand. The second door of her room led to the hallway that served as the throughway between the kitchen and the drawing room. My room stood across the hallway from hers. In the stillness of the dusk, I could hear her snoring as I ironed the cotton capris that I wore that day. A mahogany grandfather clock, tall and erect in one corner of the drawing room, let out five baritone bongs. Through my bedroom window, enormous palm trees with rough barks and expansive leaves lay motionless. Next door, Miss Leila's cock sang, "cockle-doodle-do" in his attempt to awaken the sleepy corpses of the village for the start of a new day. Although I unplugged the iron and placed it on the concrete windowsill, Mami came into my room for a second time, asking whether I remembered to unplug it. "Yeeees, Mami," I urged, frustrated that she did not believe me the first time. I did not consider for one moment what the iron represented to her. She needed to know that my carelessness would never leave her homeless again. She needed to know that my carelessness would not result in the pain and devastation that the fire caused the first time. She needed to know that, but I was too impatient to realize it then.

Mami lived in Whiteland for most of her life. The road leading into the village wakes us up in the morning and lulls us to sleep at night. It is the only way into and out of the village. And although Daddy could no longer see, he had a keen sense of everything that was happening on the compound and in the community. Somehow, all of these memories are as familiar to me as I am to myself. But what makes Whiteland home is not its geography, but its people. Fahey Street runs perpendicular to Poonah Road. The homes of approximately eighty families are nestled between large citrus and mango trees. "Neighbour" is a South Asian or, as we say in Trinidad, an Indian woman who lives at the very back of the street with her husband and two children. Her daughter Rosalind is married and lives in Princes Town. Her son, not as lucky, is a math teacher and still lives at home, even in his early forties. This is not peculiar where we live. Children have no need to leave their parents at the age of eighteen as they do in Canada. It is common for us to live with our parents until they pass on. It is also common for two to three generations to live in a single household. Elderly grandparents and great-grandparents play an important role in Trinidadian culture and we do not discard them when they grow old.

We were raised to know that children are responsible for their parents and at a very young age; we were exposed to the cycle of life whereby the elderly pass on, sometimes right in our midst. As children, we were never shielded from death, only the ailments that lead to it. We were exposed to death as a function of being alive. And although as a young child I knew that no one lives forever, I could not see the grown-up me without Mami. I simply couldn't fathom it.

Neighbour is an excellent cook. On each of my trips home she prepared curried red mangoes for me to bring back to Canada. She cooked it the night before I left and wrapped the smouldering hot fruit in brown paper with layers and layers of aluminum foil. The mango is then frozen solid to ensure that it makes its way to Canada without leaking in my suitcase. The red mango is made with brown sugar that is manufactured on the island. If I stopped to think about how much sugar the dish is made of, I wouldn't eat it. Instead, I dream about its skin melting in my mouth, each fleshy slice staining my thumb and index finger when I remove it from the messy mound that must be thawed in the microwave.

After all these years I don't know Neighbour's first name. As children, we were never allowed to call "big people" by their first names anyway, so learning her name would have been futile. Children in Caribbean households are raised so strictly. I imagine that this is due to the colonial remnants of British rule on the island, but I am not sure where this idea comes from. As children, we were taught that we must be seen and not heard. We could never swear or talk back to adults as Canadian children do. Mami made sure that I sat like a lady, ate properly, and used my manners. She taught me about being feminine. She loved the fact that I wore makeup and we always bonded over lipstick. Mami reminded me that I needed to dress nicely each time I left the home. She taught me everything that she herself did as a woman and I modelled myself after her example.

With her stocky build and short hair, Neighbour has the most beautiful green eyes. She is known for cooking authentic Indian dishes and always invited Mami to her annual Hindu "prayers," to pay homage to the gods Vishnu and Krishna. Prayers are the equivalent of a religious ceremony where friends and family gather in fellowship with each other. Neighbour prepared dhal and roti, curried goat, sahina, pumpkin and curry channa, and potato. Served on large fig leaves, we used our fingers to eat, never knives, spoons, or forks. Mami and Neighbour got on well and were fond of each other.

Miss Leila's family lived next door, right on Poonah Road. She died a few years back, but is alive and well in everyone's mind. Miss Leila was Mami's best friend. She lived hard and died young, drinking, smoking, and cursing on a daily basis for everyone to hear. Miss Leila visited Mami each morning. They sat and ate bake and pumpkin or some other breakfast dish, gossiping and talking about things too juicy for us to hear. They quickly shooed us away if we came within earshot of their conversation. Miss Leila was mixed-race, Black and Indian. Her children were either Black or mixed-race depending on who their father was. But in Trinidad, we never say "Black" and still use the term "Negro."

Miss Leila's family reflected that many families in Trinidad were interracial, Indian and Black, or culturally diverse in some way. I remember when she and her family built their house on the vacant lot beside ours. One of her babies, I can't remember which one it was, wore a soaking wet diaper and he ate the duck droppings that were scattered throughout the yard, his teeth dark green from the poop as he enjoyed his discovery. Right after Miss Leila and Mr. Lawrence built their house on the lot, I remember Mami meeting Miss Leila near it, offering her things that she needed for the home and letting her know that she was available if Miss Leila needed anything. I saw the start of their friendship and witnessed its development over the years. However, our families were from different social-class backgrounds.

I was friends with Miss Leila's eldest daughter Diane. Daddy warned me that I would get a spanking if he ever caught me playing with her.

Diane was three years older than me. One day I overheard him telling Mami that she "already had vice" and that under no circumstances should I be under her influence and Mami agreed. Although I did not know what "vice" was, I knew enough to never cross him. Daddy did not speak often, but when he did, we listened. I was on the receiving end of several spankings from him in the past, always with a whip that he picked from a thin tree with wispy branches. The whip blazed my skinny dark brown legs. I jumped up and down with each stinging lash, trying to escape the pain. "Listen...lash...next time...lash...when I tell you not to go by...lash, lash, lash!"

But while Mami was busy cooking and Daddy was at work, I stole away and met Diane by the wooden fence that Daddy and Mr. Lawrence erected years after they moved to Whiteland. The fence was our secret place. It separated us as rich and poor, the "haves" and the "have-nots." We laughed and shared stories about boys or lip gloss. Diane made me feel special and would often recount events from her days at school. I always knew that my speaking to her was risky. At any given time I could be caught by one of my aunts who might tell on me. They might even spank me themselves. It was never safe. The threat of a spanking came from all directions and from all generations. One day, while Diane and I were huddled in luscious secrecy, I spotted the black railings of Daddy's Mitsubishi pickup truck coming towards us. They reminded me of a deer's antlers. Without so much as a goodbye, I made a 100-metre dash towards our house, stepping over rocks and debris in the yard. I ran to Aunty Marian's place looking for shelter and praying that Daddy did not see me.

Diane had the skin colour of caramel and long silky braids that extended past her shoulders. Her long slender legs extended for miles out of her athletic frame. I admired and looked up to her, unable to see into her future the way that Daddy could. She was unlike my two younger cousins with whom I lived. At the time, I considered them uninteresting and annoying in the way that older sisters take younger siblings for granted.

On my trip to Trinidad in 2011, Diane visited me when she heard I was in town. Now a mother of three, she seemed unhappy. Her face bore the mark of a woman disappointed with life. She looked the same to me, except the innocence had vanished from her face and there were no remaining signs of her youth as I remembered it. I wondered for a moment how I looked to her. I heard that her brother Dexter was a famous football player on the island. On a visit to my Uncle Raphael's house, approximately two kilometres from where we lived, I spotted him as he drove by on the main road in an unknown car. I barely recognized him, but I squinted and called out to him. "Ey, Dexter, how you doin' boy?" in my best Trini twang. Dexter exposed pearly white teeth and a smile that registered his appreciation for seeing me once again after so many years. As children, my two cousins and I played with Diane, Dexter, and her brother Fat Boy. We played marbles, rounders, catch, and hide-and-go-seek. Seeing them again brought back tender memories.

Mami brought us sponge cake and Coke as we sat in the living room chatting. She and Diane exchanged pleasantries and Mami asked about her children and knew each by their name. Diane shared that she hoped to make her way to Canada one day, even though she couldn't afford the trip. She told me that she wanted to leave Trinidad to work as a nanny in Montreal. Mami knew that I might be able to give Diane advice about living in Canada and seemed pleased that we were connecting again. Diane did not seem to have all of the details worked out in her mind's eye and I could not find the words to convince her that she had. We both knew that it would never happen, but we sat together, wishfully thinking for a moment because that is what she needed. As a friend, I owed that to her.

Our parents can see things that we cannot envision in our youth. They are our compasses and our guides throughout life. They help us navigate complicated roadmaps and shield us from falling into the ditch. Daddy saw something that I was too young to see. We often do not appreciate their wisdom until we are much older or they are no longer with us.

As a childhood friend, I was happy to indulge Diane in her fantasy. I suspended my knowledge about the reality of the matter because I didn't have the heart to tell her that Canada was not what she thought it was. I thought it would be selfish of me to ruin her dream. Instead, I smiled politely, shook my head and thanked the heavens for the many blessings I had, recognizing that my life could have turned out like hers.

We knew that Mami was not well, but we were unprepared for her passing. No one is ever prepared for death. Mami was in and out of hospital the previous year for high blood pressure and other ailments that will forever remain unnamed. As a child growing up in Trinidad, my family members rarely uttered words such as "cancer" or "brain tumour." Adults simply died of "something" that they had. I am not sure what Mami died from, but I remember Aunty Juliet saying that she found it strange that the liquid from the IV that was placed into her arm flowed at a rapid speed and that she was concerned. This is unsurprising though. When Mami was alive, she stated emphatically that San Fernando General is where people go to die and we were instructed to never take her there if ever she fell ill. I remember well the day when Mami learned that a young woman from the Whiteland had passed on. The girl was eighteen years old and drank Gramoxone, a deadly poison. Mami was taken aback and said, "Who dead? Eh... You mean dat yung ghul dead? Eh, eh, eh eh, eh. Lawd." As a child, it seemed as though people died despite never having been sick. I remember the look of shock in Mami's weary eyes as she struggled to hide the blow that the sudden news gave her. As children, we were shielded from the complexities of illness, even as we were exposed to the realities of death.

Children in Trinidadian culture are rarely invited into adult conversations, at least not in the same way as Canadian children are. Aunty Marian and Mami spoke in patois, a made-up language of their creation, when they didn't want us to know what they were saying. If ever a juicy topic was raised, we were under strict orders to, "Go an' play outside!" "Outside," or the outdoors, was a coded term for, "We need privacy." Discursively, it delineated adulthood from childhood, women from girls.

It established spatial boundaries for what could only be uttered within the borderland of the home, rather than the public space of the yard or the porch. Playing "outside" also meant that we could never learn the names for illnesses such as invasive ductal carcinoma, leukemia, or some other medical conditions that guarantee bad medical news.

THAT MORNING, after receiving the devastating news of Mami's passing, I walked around in what felt like a haze. I called my Aunty Linda. She lives in Brooklyn and works as a nanny for a wealthy family in Manhattan's Upper East Side. Between phone calls, I made travel arrangements. I tried calling home, but the line was busy and I could not get through, even after trying repeatedly for over an hour. When I was finally able to connect with Aunty Juliet her voice sounded worn. She and I spoke around midnight the night before. Aunty Juliet called me from the hospital and gave me the chance to speak to Mami one last time. My throat ached and I held back the tears that were fighting desperately for release. I could hardly speak and kept repeating, "Thank you," "thank you," "thank you." I needed to thank Aunty Juliet for knowing deep down that I desperately needed to speak to Mami and for giving me the opportunity to spend those last moments with her.

When I spoke to Mami the night before her passing, it was past 11:00 p.m. I found it strange that I was receiving a call that late in the night, but Aunty Juliet had already alerted us that Mami was taken to hospital after falling near the kitchen. Mami could hardly speak, but I made her laugh. Whenever I called home, I made it my business to make her laugh. Mami often picked up the second phone in our kitchen while Daddy spoke to me from the telephone in his bedroom. She never wanted to miss anything that I said. I spoke to her gently and begged her to wait for me. Her voice was weak and I was afraid. I reassured her that I was coming home. I told her that my flight was booked and that I had already bought all the things she liked. I promised her that we would go to San Fernando to "tear food," which made her chuckle. I told her how much I loved her, over and over again. "Right...right, right," she answered and I could tell that she was smiling. I could hear her smile as she took what felt like her final breaths. But even at that moment, I didn't think that I would never hear her voice again.

Those final moments with Mami rotated constantly in my head. When Aunty Juliet passed the phone to Daddy and I heard his voice, the wailing started again, as much as I tried to suppress it. I tried to keep my composure, but I felt like I was losing control. Daddy was the only person who knew what I was going through. He was my father and understood my special bond with Mami. But on hearing me cry, Daddy scolded me. He told me that I needed to be strong for him and with his admonition, I settled and began to breathe through my nose. I took comfort in his voice. He was all that I had left.

As we spoke, I explained to Daddy that Mami gave me her two prayer books when I visited in 2011. The first was *St. Anthony's Everyday Companion*. The worn burgundy cover reads, "A manual of devotion for Tuesdays and other needs of St. Anthony's clients." The picture shows a Catholic saint with a small child, perhaps an angel, in his hands. It smelt of old paper that was well used, but intact. The second book was *Pray the Rosary* and showed a picture of a serene woman wearing a white head covering. Her hands were clasped and her eyes were closed. Below the image, it read, "Ideal for Rosary Novenas," which are special prayers recited in the Roman Catholic faith, especially in a time of need. I told Daddy that Mami gave me the two books the morning that Eric and I left for Canada, which he found surprising. Mami used both books for praying each day and never parted with them. She was so attached to both books that as children we knew never to tamper with them in any way or remove them from her bedside table.

It was 2011 and Kennedy and I were in the front yard getting ready to return to Canada. Daddy sat in his favourite spot on the veranda and Eric was busy rolling our suitcases to Uncle Raphael's car. Mami,

Aunty Juanita and I walked towards the back of the house and stood near the car as our luggage was being loaded into the trunk. Mami then stretched out her hands and gave me both books. She was silent. She didn't say anything to me, but looked at me without smiling. I looked deeply into her eyes, as if to say, "Do you really want to part with these?" In hindsight, Mami's gift began to make sense. I searched my memory bank, desperate for answers. The morning after speaking to Mami for the last time, I awoke and found both books on the floor near my bed, even though they were securely in my drawer the night before. And as I bent down to retrieve them, I noticed a tube of lipstick that had fallen beneath the bed and nightstand. I picked it up and added it to the stash of makeup that I was amassing in preparation for my trip.

THE THOUGHT OF TRAVELLING home to Trinidad for a funeral during parang season felt bittersweet. The fact that Mami passed during her favourite time of year was not lost on us, the Jack clan. What a blow. I felt cheated. I was stunned. But Mami's passing at Christmas time reminded me of the year when I received my first Black doll. It was Christmas morning in 1982 and nothing had prepared me for the devastation I experienced at receiving *me*, when I knew to my core that Black was not beautiful. To this day, I am unsure when this feeling started for me. While these words were never spoken to me directly, I managed to solve this puzzle based on the plethora of information that I received from my family and Trinidadian culture in general. In the late 1970s to mid-1980s, I saw images of myself on local television, but never American channels, which rarely depicted my life on a Caribbean island. There were two television stations on our black and white TV. The only shows that featured characters that looked like us were *The Jeffersons, Sanford and Son, Diff'rent Strokes*, and *Good Times*, all of which depicted the lives of African Americans who were struggling to carve a life for themselves in the United States. On American television, to be Black meant to be African American and no other Black identities existed. With the exception of *The Jeffersons*, Black characters were depicted as desperately poor and this did not reflect our upwardly mobile, middle-class aspirations. And although Daddy and Mami were not university educated, we enjoyed a more comfortable lifestyle than most people in our village. As a child, I heard my aunts and uncle saying that whenever Black characters were depicted on television, they were rarely seen as anything but impoverished and on the island we knew that there were families who were also wealthy and middle-class. And although we were living on an island, the fact that Trinidad had oil meant that the poverty shown of Black lives in the USA did not reflect our life or the lives of our family and friends on the island.

One of few positive representations of Blackness came from the nation's Prime Minister Dr. Eric Williams, a historian and Harvard grad with expertise in Caribbean history. I felt pride in knowing that the leader of our country looked like the men in my family. And although he was not as dark as me, he was Black. In my family, my aunts often made jokes that suggested that my dark skin was undesirable; however, this was true of Caribbean culture in general. I never heard Mami explicitly speaking about my dark skin, but if ever my aunts made jokes about skin colour, she often rebuked them, perhaps knowing that my feelings might be hurt. The one thing that Mami emphasized, however, was that I should wear red lipstick because darker colours were unsuitable for my complexion. Mami went to great lengths to ensure that I wore bright colours in my choice of clothing. I heard over and over again that because I was so dark, I couldn't wear black. Reds, yellows, oranges, and pastels were best for me, or at least those are the colours that became imprinted in my mind's eye as being suitable for me because my dark skin was viewed as a detraction from a woman's beauty, from my beauty.

The dark skin of my new doll was incongruent with my own belief system, even at such a tender age. What I remember is that I had asked for a doll that Christmas and I assumed that a *doll* meant a *white* one. At the time I lived with Aunt Marian, Uncle Reagy, and their two daughters. Aunty Marian promised me that if I scored high in "test" at school, as I had been doing consistently for years, I would be given a doll on Christmas morning. I savoured each morsel that she spoke and I dreamt at night about what the doll could possibly be. In Trinidad, our family tradition is to replace old curtains, tablecloths, doilies, and other household decorations on Christmas Eve. This renewal of the home was the promise of a new beginning that coincides with the birth of Christ. That Christmas morning my two cousins and I woke to a house that felt new. It was refreshed, with the colour orange figuring prominently throughout the living room. Aunty Marian put up a new lace curtain and a white crocheted tablecloth. The sun shone brightly through glass louvres and it was sweltering hot. I ran to the synthetic Christmas tree and retrieved the largest present that took the shape of a doll. I had been eyeing it for weeks when I was alone and out of earshot of anyone. Me and my cousins had intimate conversations about who was getting what for Christmas that year. They both knew that a new doll was the only present that I would ever want, ever.

I ripped open the present and was disappointed by the chocolate woman who stared back at me. Her skin was a café colour and her hair was jet black, with sharply cut bangs. And instead of being happy I cried, "But Aunty Marian, I wanted a white one!" I felt tricked, duped. It was not fair. How could this have happened when I specifically told her that I wanted a doll? How could she have found this Black doll when all the stores in San Fernando carried white ones? On a trip to High Street with Aunty Marian one month prior, I pointed to many pretty dolls. I could not believe that she went and did a switcheroo on me. Surely she must have known that I wanted a white doll. Its skin reminded me too much of the sand that could be found all over our yard. Its lips were painted pink and its hazel eyes sparkled under long ebony lashes. The doll was almost as tall as I was. Sure, I thought that the doll was pretty *in its own way*, but it was not white. When I articulated my displeasure, my aunt was livid.

What?...what you say?...
What you mean a white one?...

You Black!
You don't know you Black?...
It look just like you...
This is the best one for you!
Nothing wrong with this one...
You stay with that!

As she spoke, her voice faded away into the deepest crevices of my mind and I began to talk back silently, so that only the cave between my ears could hear the echoes of my wrath.

But you're not dark Aunty Marian...
You look like Mami...
You're light-skinned...
Everyone likes it.
No one makes fun of you...
She so dark eh?...she real dark...watch the smooth darkie!

Aunty Marian was the second oldest of Mami's children. With a handsome face and a stocky build, she was always the life of the party and one of the funniest people I have encountered in my life. Aunty Marian was an excellent mother. She was organized, an excellent cook, and well-loved in our community. Light-skinned, she could easily pass for biracial herself and may not have known the pain that being dark-skinned felt like.

And in that instant when my protest was shut down, I was left to deal with the reality of my Blackness, holding it as it were, in the palm of my hands. I tried to be happy. I tried to think about its positive attributes. I tried to love it, but in that moment, I couldn't. I tried to think that Aunty Marian and Uncle Reagy spent a considerable amount on the gift, simply by its size. They must have spent hundreds. I was also aware that my cousins did not receive such a large present and that they often gave me more than their own children, which wasn't fair, but it is the truth. I was selfish and felt guilty. Defeated, I resigned myself to the fact that my big Christmas present was not what I wanted. To make myself feel better, I retrieved a brown comb from our wooden chest of drawers located in the bedroom that I shared with my cousins.

I sat on the chair in the living room and began to play with its long hair. The cushion was soft and I pinned her plastic torso between my knees to ensure that she would not fall to the ground. I rationalized that even though the doll was Black, at least it had long hair. In fact, its hair was the primary reason why I wanted it in the first place, and as I slid the comb between the silky nylon fibres of a scalp that was littered with holes made for each hair follicle, my disappointment slowly began to fade. I played with the doll quietly while my cousins milled about in their excitement beside me. I played with its hair knowing that it would be the only doll that I would receive until next Christmas, if at all. I played with its hair, fantasizing that perhaps my hair would be that long and silky one day. I played with its hair, but I did not love it.

Track 4:
BEOWULF RETURNS HOME

Soundtrack:

De Verdad
Daisy Voisin

Esto Se Paso
Daisy Voisin

Sak Pase
Krosfyah ft. Edwin Yearwood

Marajhin
Mighty Sparrow

Savannah Grass
Kes the Band

Landslide
Fleetwood Mac

No Roots
Alice Merton

The Chokin' Kind
Joss Stone

Kind of Blue
Miles Davis

If Tomorrow Never Comes
Garth Brooks

Hero
Mariah Carey

She's Royal
Tarrus Riley

A FEW DAYS AFTER I received the news of Mami's passing, a cold front moved into Kingston and ice was everywhere. I was desperate to finish marking the final papers for the course, which would enable me to focus on my trip. And because universities do not mourn the dead, it was business as usual at Queen's. I was given two days of bereavement leave. Two days to mourn the loss of my mother. The good news was that the semester was almost over and because I was not a full-time faculty member, I was able to travel to Trinidad for at least two weeks to keep wake with my family.

I knew I had to face the inevitable and tried my best to keep busy. Calling home and not being able to hear Mami's voice on the other end of the line felt strange. It was the first time in my life when I needed her and she was not there. I did not know what to expect. I wasn't sure what our house would feel like without her. I could not remember a time in my life when she was not in our house. This is what loss feels like. At first, the loss becomes apparent through the small things and over time, the more profound realizations come to bear as the shock sets in.

The experience of Mami's loss began to take shape almost immediately, at first physically, then emotionally, but also culturally in terms of what Mami meant to our family and our community in Whiteland. Eric sensed I was in a fragile state and did his best to comfort me. He made me tea. He brought my suitcase up to the second floor after collecting dust in our basement since our previous trip. He made Kennedy's lunch and warned me to brace myself for what I was about to experience.

I booked my ticket on Caribbean Airlines. Having to deal with the online booking was not something that I appreciated. Once on a trip to Trinidad, I made the mistake of booking with Air Transat, a discount carrier, who only served peanuts on a five-hour trip. I will never trust my life with an airline who will not bother to feed their passengers. Carefully packing my suitcase, I looked over the items I had bought for Mami, but the gifts did not make sense now: Cabotine de Grès perfume from France, a Fossil leather handbag with many pockets for all of Mami's receipts, a brand new pair of flip-flops, a compact powder by Guerlain in a terracotta shade that matched her complexion, medicines, and a MAC lipstick. I visited the MAC makeup counter at the Cataraqui Mall. It was tucked in a corner of The Bay, right beside the exit that leads to the rest of the mall. The sales associate recognized me instantly and greeted me with a smile. I told her that I hoped to purchase lipstick for my mother and she recommended the colour Au Chaud. I knew that Mami would love it, a matte red-orange hue with no shimmer, shine, or gimmick.

I LEFT FOR TRINIDAD on Tuesday, December 10, 2013 and yearned for my home in Trinidad, but I did not look forward to travelling from Kingston to Toronto, or having to take the long overnight flight. I took the train from Kingston to Union Station and a shuttle bus from the Royal York hotel to Pearson International. It was dingy and slushy outside and my ankle boots were soaking wet. I could feel my toes becoming more and more numb as I waited for the driver to place my suitcase into the cabin below. Once on the bus, I relaxed a bit and my feet began to thaw in the warmth of my seat. I was happy to be one step closer to home, as much as my tummy performed somersaults and capsized to and fro in anticipation. More than anything, I looked forward to leaving Canada, even for a short time, to feel like myself again in Trinidad. At the airport, I checked in at the Caribbean Airlines kiosk with no fuss. My bags were tagged and loaded onto the carousel that somehow leads to the plane. Once complete, I went through the security and headed to my gate since I was a tad early. Sitting at the gate, I took out an *InStyle* magazine to read, but I could not focus. I kept thinking about Mami.

After boarding the plane and getting settled into my window seat, a Black woman wearing a red dress sat beside me. She smiled with kind eyes and we exchanged pleasantries, but I did not feel like talking. Once we were in the air, I looked out the window to the starry galaxy below and began reminiscing about the times I shared with Mami. One of my early memories of Mami is of Mother's Day. I must have only been six or seven years old. At school, the teachers taught us a song and I sang it for her when I arrived home that evening. Mami was always busy cooking, but that day she sat in her chair and listened intently as I sang, my voice angelic and pure.

Mami's eyes danced in amusement and love. A singer herself, she enjoyed watching us sing, dance, and perform. When I kissed and hugged her after the performance, I knew that she was happy. Mami asked questions about the teacher who taught us the song and about how long we were practising it at school the week before. It was a tender moment and after all these years, the song never left me. At the time, I didn't pay much attention to the meaning of the words because I loved the melody more than the lyrics. As an adult, I can see now how mature the theme of the song was and that I could easily sing this song to Aunty Erroline or Aunty Marian and the meaning still rings true.

Another memory that remains with me is the day Mami took me to San Fernando to buy a Marvin Gaye record. It was 1982 and I was nine years old. Although this memory is less vivid, I remember Mami holding my hand on crowded High Street and leading me to the record store. We entered the shop and she approached the sales associate at the counter. He looked down at us from his elevated chair. Mami could not remember the name of the song, so she sang the chorus. The song was all over the charts. I remember Dick Clark on *American Top 40* revealing to us that the song had reached number one in America, but for the life of me, I could not understand why Mami mumbled the words to the song. Back then, I didn't know what "sexual healing" was and Mami was sure never to repeat the phrase loudly while in my presence. Instantly recognizing the catchy melody, the associate retrieved a 45 record from the stack immediately behind his head. Satisfied, Mami placed the record into one of the shopping bags that she always took with her from our home.

My mind also wandered to the time Mami slapped me in my face for spitting on my cousin Merlynda. It was the only time I remember being spanked by Mami. But it wasn't true. Merlynda and I were playing and fighting, as we were accustomed to. We were outside in the yard at the back of the old house near the large mango tree and Mami was milling about in the yard. We were only two years apart, me being the oldest grandchild and Merlynda the second oldest. And although I did not spit on her, Merlynda cried out to Mami as though I did and told on me. In an instant, Mami ran over to where I was and slapped me dead in my face. Stunned at the injustice of the bold-faced lie, I looked at Mami in shock and burned with anger. Mami scolded me, "Don't you ever spit at another person in your life ever again!" Although I understood why Mami was so swift to punish me, I thought it was unfair that she never asked me whether it was true. Moments later, after my cousin and I were out of earshot from Mami and the rest of my family, I attacked her. I punched her in the belly as hard as I could and tried to rip the cornrows from her head. She cried out in pain but I did not stop. When the attack was over, Merlynda ran away carrying even more "news" on me the second time. I rationalized that she needed to learn a lesson and that if Mami was going to be disappointed in me, it would have to be for the truth and not a lie. After replacing this memory with happier ones, I fell asleep and woke up approximately one hour before we landed at the airport.

CALLING BOTH TRINIDAD and Canada home is no different from loving two children. I am unable to choose one over the other. I need both. As a second-generation Canadian, I never feel Trini enough. I never feel Canadian enough either. When I go "back home" to Trinidad, it feels as though I've just put on my favourite Ralph Lauren sweater. Its soft cotton ridges are warm and fluffy from frequent washing and lots of fabric softener. I can be myself in Trinidad. I can be Black. I am not out of place. Everyone looks like me. I understand my place. I understand the norms, the customs, and the things that people value. I am understood in Trinidad as well and I can relax, even if it's for a few moments. Going home to the Caribbean provides a lifeline from Canadian culture which is designed to suck the life out of me.

As a child I attended Vos Government School in Gasparillo, near Texaco, now called Petrotrin. Each time I hear the word "Petrotrin," my brain expunges it and replaces it with its former name. Although most of my school was made up of "Negro" and "Indian" classmates, there was one white girl whose parents were from Canada, I believe. She was pale and had long, flowing hair. There were also Asian students, some who were mixed-race, and some who were Panyol, like Mami. My feeling of belonging in Trinidad has more to do with feeling a sense of belonging in a culture where I am not made to feel like the villain—in the media, walking down the street, in school, at the bank, in fancy restaurants. In Trinidad, people don't treat me with scorn even before I utter a word.

Growing up, even though there were racial tensions between South Asians and Black people on the island, especially along political lines, I still managed to see Black doctors and lawyers, police officers and entrepreneurs, taxi drivers and musicians. Being Black in Trinidad was more expansive than what it means to be Black in Canada. There was more complexity and room to play with my identity. I was not reduced to fitting into neat but dangerous stereotypes: the athlete, the musician...the criminal. Aunty Gemma's husband was a chemist and there was nothing strange about him being a Black man in the field of science. I remember Daddy telling me as a child that there was nothing I couldn't do and that I could be anything I wanted to be. What a gift. He must have known that I would need that self-assurance in Canada where Black skin is relegated to the bottom rung of an invisible but tightly structured caste system. I am sure that Daddy knew this when he uttered those words to me.

When I go home to Trinidad, I do not question whether I belong there. I need that feeling of knowing in my life. I need to feel that sense of belonging. As a Black woman living in Canada, issues surrounding my identity are never resolved. They are always in play...always on the table, threatening to wreak havoc, especially when I least expect it. This becomes tiring, day in and day out. I say this even though I love my country deeply. I love Canada, but Canada does not love me. It is an unrequited love at its best. I am not trying to romanticize how my identity plays out in Trinidad, because tensions between South Asians and Black people are complicated in Trinidadian culture as well; I grew up listening to my family members speaking about South Asians who did not like Black people or that some South Asian families would disown a daughter for marrying a Black man. The difference is in Trinidad, after the pulling and tugging between the races and cultures is over, I know that I can find safety and comfort in being from there. My people are from there. We belong to the land and the land belongs to us. There is no one telling me to go back where I came from because I am from there.

I don't know of one Black person in all of Canada who is pleased to be asked by a white person, "Where are you from?" This rude and vulgar intrusion happens over and over again, causing psychic pain and emotional harm. I wish white people would stop it, but their white privilege won't stand for it. They will fight us every step of the way. When I am asked this question, I find myself literally "standing on guard" in my attempt to lay claim to this land as a Black woman who was born here. But it really doesn't matter. My being born in Canada matters very little, precisely because I am Black. I watch as Canadians embrace "newcomers" from other countries, even as we treat Indigenous Peoples with a disgrace too disgusting for words. I watch as "newcomers" who are white or white passing are treated better than me, because of my Black skin. I am always relegated to the back of the bus and nothing much has really changed.

These days there appears to be so much chatter about Blackness in Canada, especially after the murder of George Floyd in 2020, but no one is saying anything about how race is experienced differently by different groups and it is all noise. If we are to be truthful with ourselves, we will admit that Canada has a major problem with race and an even bigger problem with its hatred of Black people. We need to be honest about what it is really like to live with Black skin in this country and this is not something that white political pundits can explain away with vague and opaque language. We need to start asking Black people what it means to be Black in Canada. We need to begin to make Black people the subjects of our own experiences rather than mere objects of equity, diversity, and inclusion.

In Canada, I am always made to feel as though I belong somewhere else. I despise it and it hurts. In perpetually being asked, "Where are you from?" I am reminded over and over again that Blackness is not *of* here. It is as though we can never belong to this country. When I am with Black friends and work colleagues, we often trade notes about the last time we were asked the offensive question. We complain. We vent in frustration, anger, and insult. We are Canadian, but we are not *believed* to be Canadian. We need to be believed. It is this act of believing that we are Canadian that matters. Canadians do not yet believe that anyone who is not white can lay claim to this land. One thing I can say for sure is that this process of believing I am truly Canadian is generations in the making. It will not happen overnight and will only begin to take shape when our hearts break for the exclusion that Black people experience here.

It is this disbelief that we are Canadian that continues to haunt us. But believing that we are Canadian cannot be legislated. It has to come from one's soul. This disbelief in my Canadianness creates a tension between how I see myself and how others see me. Most of the Black people I know resent being asked where we are from. Many of us dream of the day when we can attend a social gathering without being marked as Other in this way. We want to belong to this country. We need to belong to this country. I was born on Canadian soil, but I am not believed to be Canadian. We must pay attention to our belief systems because they prevent us from moving forward as a nation.

When we are asked, "Where are you from?" we fume. We strategize. We step forward in careful consideration like two fencers going in for the kill. We dance and pivot back and forth, angling for the right position. There is power in the act of doing the asking. The person who asks the question matters. The person asking the question discursively establishes that they *are* Canadian. In asking the question, "Where are you from?" the asker guides the conversation and sets a power imbalance in motion where I feel compelled to give a response.

But the problem also lies with me. As a Black Canadian, I continue to answer the question despite the psychic turmoil that it causes. I must take ownership of this fact and this is something I continue to grapple with.

In answering the question, "Where are you from?" I am telling the questioner that such a question is acceptable and deserving of a response. I often wonder what would happen if I switched the script and created different responses, such as:

Why do you ask?
Where are you from?
That's neither here nor there…
Lovely day out today, isn't it…
I am walking away now…

What would compel you to ask such a thing? When did *your* family arrive in Canada?...and,
If you're not Indigenous, you're actually not from here, so what gives?

The sad reality is that as a people, we do not have a collective strategy for "talking back." This is because Black communities in Canada are diverse and fragmented. We are not unified in vision or experiences. We are not a monolith. We do the best that we can in an attempt to "make it." We cope on an individual basis with each microaggression, even when we understand that it is the colour of our skin that begs the foul question in the first place, simultaneously marking us as outsider and foreigner in our own country.

What I must consider deeply is that Canada *is* my home. I must deal with what it means for me to leave my home in Canada for another home in Trinidad and to leave Trinidad to return home to Canada once again. In 2011 when Kennedy was three years old, we left Kingston for a trip to Trinidad without telling anyone in my family but Aunty Joslin in Boston. We wanted to surprise Mami. We flew into the airport on an overnight flight. Even at 5:00 a.m., the sun blazed and the humidity made me feel overdressed and uncomfortable in my pink cardigan set. After gathering our matching Briggs and Riley suitcases from the lazy carousel, Eric and I pushed past the exit doors at Piarco International Airport to a line of taxi drivers who eagerly anticipated the release of passengers aboard Caribbean Airlines Flight 711. The taxi drivers, some of whom held signs with the names "Elliot," "Velasquez," and "Garcia," called out to us, desperate to snatch our business. After leaving the building, drivers who lined the walkway inquired, "Way yuh goin'?" and "Oy" behind old Datsuns and Maximas in anticipation of the day's fare.

"Whiteland! South boy...south, pass Gasparillo," I sang back in my best Trini accent. I was exhausted and my body ached from holding Kennedy in my arms all night long. The driver yelled, "Naaah, I eh goin' dong dey." His eyes avoided mine as if to say, "That is much too far for my liking." I called out to another South Asian driver using my Trini accent again. I knew that if he detected my Canadianness he would gouge me with the fare. I lay my accent on thickly in my quest to be seen as authentically Trini and sang:

Anita: Yuh goin' up Whiteland?
Taxi Driver: I eh no way dat is.
Anita: South, boy, south! Pass, Gasparillo, it eh fah!

We continued the negotiation back and forth, he deciding whether my offer of $500.00 Trinidadian dollars would be worth his while and me convincing him that my offer was too good to pass up. The driver finally surrendered and helped Eric place our suitcases in the trunk of the car. Each suitcase was filled with gifts for Mami and Daddy: Tums for Daddy's acid reflux, Tylenol for his aches and pains, Rub A535 for the foot he complained about, Tiger Balm for Mami's arthritis, and a large jar of Arctic Ice Analgesic Gel that I picked up for a reasonable price at the Walmart out in Bayridge.

I took a large bottle of Chanel Coco Mademoiselle, Eau de Parfum for Mami. It was the second bottle that she owned. On a previous trip to Trinidad, I wore the fragrance and she liked it, so I gave her the remainder of that bottle and made a note to buy her a new one. I took striped shorts, black underwear, and colourful muscle tops for Daddy that I picked up at Target in Watertown, New York, not too far from our cottage in the 1000 Islands on the US side. For my teenage cousin Jayon, I bought Nike and Adidas clothing at Value Village. I washed them a few times and they looked brand new again. I took bags and bags of makeup: eyeshadows, lip glosses, blushes and foundations, small bottles of perfume, makeup cases, makeup brushes, and large handbags for my closest relatives.

We left the airport and sped southbound along the Solomon Hochoy Highway. Reggae music blared from the well-worn car. *She's Royal* by Tarrus Riley was at the top of the charts. The car had to be a 1985 Datsun. It was reliable and promised to take us to our destination. The seats were dark brown with beige carpets and smelled of cigarettes, stale body odour, and an artificial air freshener used to mask the offensive smells. We whizzed by hastily in the early morning sun. I admired the array of homes that lined the roadside. Some were large, colourful, and manicured to a fault. Nestled right beside them were smaller homes that were half-finished, with the drywall exposed and bricks and cement strewn in the yard. No one seemed to mind the juxtaposition of old and new, the haves and the have-nots, existing together in the Caribbean heat.

When we pulled into busy Gasparillo Junction, the cars were jammed up against each other in traffic that seemed to veer off in five different directions at once. It was utter chaos. The roads were unlined and there were no traffic lights to make sense of the bedlam. As a child, I did not see it this way, but in looking at it through Canadian eyes, I was taken aback by the melee. I knew that we needed to turn left because I recognized the white fence of my former school, Vos Government, perched on a hill straight ahead of us. To my right, I could see the large oil tanks of Petrotrin and knew that I was almost home.

"Make ah lef hyeh," I commanded the driver from the backseat. "Well how fah dis is? If I know is so far we goin', I would a neva take alyuh," he protested, angry by his miscalculation of the vast distance. We drove for one hour and were still twenty minutes away from home. Feeling his anger, I assured him, "We almos' reach…It eh fah again." The driver kissed his teeth in disgust and mumbled under his breath, making his displeasure known. The traffic in Gasparillo was still gridlocked. Black and Brown people walked everywhere. A Rastafarian walked past our car, his dark skin glistening in the sun. His dreadlocks were tied up in a large crocheted hat and it seemed as though his head disappeared into the mouth of a beautifully woven basket. He was beautiful to me.

As early as I can remember, I found Rastafarians beautiful. I remember walking to school from Aunty Marian's former house in Gasparillo, before she built the house on Daddy's lot. There were some construction workers who were building the sidewalk on the main road and among them was a tall Rastafarian man who always looked out for me. One day, he ushered me out of the rain and wiped my face with a towel. He told me to remain in the shelter until the rain passed and took care of me the way a father takes care of a child. I was taught that Rastafarians are deeply spiritual and peaceful people. Not too long ago, on my way home from Queen's in Kingston, a pickup truck pulled up beside my car and on the outside of the cargo area hung a Rastafarian plush toy. It was brown with oversized lips. Out of his mouth hung a large stick of marijuana. His brown hair and red, yellow, and green hat bobbled in the wind. It made me sick to see a Black man through the eyes of a racist. However, in seeing the beauty of the Rastafarian who stood before me, I reminded myself that I did not have to hold on to problematic constructions of who we are in Canada. I could release them from my psyche and replace them with what I know to be true.

Approximately ten minutes away from San Fernando, the drivers tried to make sense of the gridlock. Some men stuck their hands out of their cars to communicate where they intended to go. Up meant right, down meant left. The street buzzed with pedestrians who walked in all directions, even between the cars. The smell of Kentucky Fried Chicken was distinct and strong, and even at 7:00 a.m. the lineup to the restaurant spilled outside the door. Customers stood in a straight line, each eagerly awaiting their turn for that all too familiar taste.

A Muslim man dressed in a white kameez and shalwar attended his fruit stand. Mounds of apples, oranges, and grapes were heaped into vibrant apartments. We slowly passed by local shops with hand-drawn signs that sold cosmetics, clothing, and groceries. We crawled by a large storefront that sold tires. I knew that the owner was our former neighbour on Fahey Street where we lived. An old, female South Asian vendor sold doubles out of a Styrofoam container to a crowd of men and women who huddled near the stall.

We left Gasparillo and headed inland towards Whiteland. I knew the narrow winding road with no sidewalk by heart. We drove past a large cane field that was recently cleared. We came to a village called Monwash and passed several small villages on the way. Each offered mom and pop shops that sold chips and candy. But this stretch of land was rural, with no gas stations, banks, or industry to speak of. Surrounded by lush trees and thick bush, we continued along our way. The taxi driver fumed and insisted that he could go no further. I ignored him and thought about seeing Mami in a few short minutes. When we entered the vicinity of Whiteland, I asked him to slow down and suggested that he pull over to the right near the large sign for the car wash. The sign was made from an old metal car door and was hung up on the electrical pole just off the main road. Aunty Marian owned the land and rented the space to a young entrepreneur who paved the dirt and created a bustling business in only a matter of years.

The taxi driver made a right from the main road onto Fahey Street and another immediate right into the gates of our compound. He was visibly upset and didn't look me in the eye when I got out of the car. I stretched my hand to award him his well-earned fare. He took the money but was not happy. I thanked him and we parted ways. I was relieved to be home after such a long journey. He was happy to leave the rural expanse of financial nothingness and return to the promise of financial gain in Port of Spain.

When we arrived home, Mami opened the back door, prompted by the sound of the car's engine. I called out to her and announced our arrival. Dumbfounded, she didn't have the words to make sense of our presence. I greeted her on the back porch and told her that we were tired after having travelled all night long. Mami then scolded me for coming home without telling her and asked me how I made it all that way without any help. With Kennedy asleep on my shoulder, I laughed and reminded her that I knew where I lived and that I could make it home with my eyes closed.

Track 5:
A BIRD IN THE HOUSE

Soundtrack:

Sereno Sereno
Daisy Voisin

Dancing Queen
Abba

September
Earth, Wind & Fire

Brown Eyed Girl
Van Morrison

Could You Be Loved
Bob Marley & the Wailers

All Night Long (All Night)
Lionel Richie

Night Nurse
Gregory Isaacs

Jesus at the Center
Israel Houghton

Misty Blue
Dorothy Moore

THE FIRST TIME I took Eric to Trinidad was in 2005, the year after we got married. George W. Bush was the president of the United States and Kennedy was not yet born. I wanted him to experience Trinidadian culture first-hand. He had travelled all over Africa, Europe, and South America and took many trips with his father, Michael Davies, on The Archangel, a C&C Custom 67 recreational keelboat that moored destinations such as the Galápagos Islands, Fiji islands, and Bermuda for a total of approximately 90,000 miles. During our visit, Eric had to get used to different gender norms, our Trini patois, and the hierarchy that existed in our family with Daddy as the patriarch.

Upon meeting Daddy for the first time, Eric extended his hand and called him "Patrick." He was immediately scolded by Mami who explained, "That is Daddy to you!" From that moment on, Eric called him "Daddy," even though he found it strange and uncomfortable at first. The very next morning while sitting on the porch together, "Daddy" rolled off his tongue as they discussed the start of land development and home building business and each of the three residential subdivisions that he and his business partner John Armitage were working on. Daddy listened intently and asked detailed questions about pouring concrete, laying the foundation for houses, hiring subtrades, and selling the finished homes. Fascinated by the scope of Eric's business operation and the sheer volume of homes that they were able to build in one season, Daddy hung on to Eric's every word and I watched in silence as a father spoke to his son. The difference in skin colour, age, and experience was washed away by what matters to men the most: their work. Daddy often looked up to the sky in the way that he did when he tried to understand something complicated. They spoke for hours. During breaks in their chats, Daddy called out to me asking me whether I had fixed Eric's breakfast and whether I had given him Carib or a Vat 19 rum, even at 9:00 a.m. Eric enjoyed the freedom surrounding alcohol and the laid-back nature of island life. However, he was forbidden from interacting with women in the kitchen.

In our family, men do not cook or do so only if their wives are away in America or Canada, working as nannies or home care aides, in order to "send money" back home. And although most women worked in the home when I was a child, Aunty Marian often drove a taxi to make extra money, and Aunty Juliet and Aunty Erroline owned a clothing store in San Fernando for a short time. When Aunty Gemma was alive, I often sent her toiletries in large boxes that she sold to friends and neighbours. During one phone call before she passed in 2015, she shared with me that she made the equivalent of $250.00 Canadian dollars in one day selling the products to her valued customers on High Street in San Fernando.

One night, Eric and I were sleeping in bed. It was 3:00 a.m., and out of nowhere, I heard the piercing sound of the mandolin, clear, distinct, and haunting. I heard someone shaking the chac chac and the singers sang, "Sereno sereno, sereno sera, Estos son seronos, de la madruga." I pushed on Eric's shoulder to wake him up. "Wake up, parang is here." Somewhat in a daze, he could not make sense of my words. "Wake up, brush your teeth quickly, and get dressed. Parang is here. We need to host the musicians." Eric looked at me quizzically and began to hustle. "Parang reach!" I shouted loudly to the rest of the house in the stillness of the dark. I ran to Mami and Daddy's room to urge them to wake up. I then called out to Eric asking whether he was decent and had his pyjamas on.

Back in my room, I got dressed hurriedly and explained to Eric that parang is the equivalent of Christmas carolling in Canada, confused as he was about the revelry of the full parang band who played gaily in the living room, demanding our hospitality. I hadn't explained to him what parang was and gave him a short précis of what it was as I hurried along: we must prepare food for the musicians who had been travelling for several days; the musicians grace our home with their music and in return, we feed them food and spirits, provide a place to sleep, clean clothing, and a warm shower, if needed. In preparing to host the band, Mami and I were in a frenzy. Mami heated up stewed chicken and rice in the microwave. It was her best and most famous dish. I put out Old Oak rum, Johnny Walker Scotch, Carib beer, bottles of Coke, and a filled ice bucket that we bought from the gas station in Gasparillo. I also laid out drinking glasses, peanuts, napkins, and slices of sponge cake while Mami got the rest of the meal ready. When Eric entered our living room and saw the musicians singing and playing, he was moved to tears. I wasn't prepared for parang's impact on his soul. For so long, I took parang for granted. Parang was such an everyday part of my life that it never dawned on me its sweet sound could move someone in that way.

In an instant, Mami pulled Eric onto the makeshift dance floor. A table and chair had been cleared to make room for the fête. They twirled and danced to the sound of the bass, the maracas making their scratchy percussion sound while the cuatro and mandolin pierced through our hearts. And Mami cried, "Opa, Opa," enjoying her first dance with Eric, a mother with her son. The musicians sang as they played. They were weary but enjoyed watching us. We drank up the sounds of Christmas in our home and on our island. One of the musicians gave me the maracas and I began to sing and play, growing up as I did with parang in my blood. I love to play the maracas. The musicians played, ate, and danced with us until the sun came up. They then said their goodbyes in a crowded Lexus and made their way to a friend's house not too far from where we lived.

We love parang. We lean on parang. We need parang to make it through the difficult times. Parang holds our family together. As a child, I watched Mami and Daddy sing with each parang band who visited us. With adult eyes, I can see Daddy singing lead with one parang band who visited our home. He is leading the band with his eyes closed and the Spanish rolling off his tongue. I was so proud that he was my dad. With a cup in his left hand and a large bottle of rum in his right, he poured the alcohol on the floor to bless the house. At that moment, he was the most beautiful man in the world to me, tall, dark, handsome, and talented. Years later Eric shared with me that he had never before seen such a display of love as he saw with parang in Trinidad.

M Y OVERNIGHT FLIGHT to Trinidad from Toronto was hassle-free but the queasy feeling in my tummy was still there. When the plane touched down on Trinidadian soil after the long flight, I breathed a sigh of relief and thanked my Lord for his provision for a safe and hassle-free flight. Aunty Juliet picked me up from the airport with Uncle Wayne. They asked me how my flight was and whether I wanted to stop off in San Fernando to buy some breakfast. They took me to a small café in Gasparillo. I bought bake and saltfish and ate it in the back of the car. Trinidad was exactly as I remembered it. The sounds, the smells, the people. I began to breathe deeply and freely because I was home at last. I was out of the cold and in a place where I could breathe.

The road between Gasparillo and Whiteland was exactly what I had come to expect. Soca music blared from the radios in nearby cars. Commercials announced upcoming fêtes in San Fernando that we were warned not to miss. When we finally arrived home to Whiteland, I entered our home cautiously. Something was missing...something didn't feel right. The house smelled like Mami and I took comfort in that. I could not shake the empty feeling that her void created. Aunty Juliet opened the apartment where I would be staying. The apartment was an addition made to the side of our house that was the farthest away from Mami and Daddy's bedroom. I immediately visited Daddy, who lay on his bed, quietly listening to the buzz of my arrival. I kissed him as I always do and we chatted about my flight. But my heart was heavy. We made small talk and I reminded myself that I could not cry. By the time of my arrival, Aunty Marian had already flown in from Boston and was staying at her house next door. Uncle Joseph was on his way from England. No one knew if Aunty Joslin, estranged as she was from most of us, would make it. I heard gossip that Mami begged her to come home weeks before she died, but she refused. Over a nine-day period, we anticipated the arrival of siblings, cousins, nieces, and nephews. No one knew whether my biological mother would attend as the story of her arrival kept changing with each phone call she made to Aunty Juliet.

That night our home hummed with excitement for the wake. A wake in Canada is nothing in comparison to a wake in Trinidad, which felt more like a feast or a wedding. Neighbours dropped by to spend time with us, often bringing bags of food: roti, pelau, freshly baked bread, and a host of South Asian dishes like pholourie and chutney, curried chicken, baigan choka, curried channa, and potatoes. Extended family members from Mami and Daddy's side of the family chipped in with the cooking. For breakfast, I ate my favourite dishes: bake and pumpkin, and bread and cheese. We often had rice and stew chicken for lunch. The small kitchen was swarmed with food on the countertops, stovetop, and the large white freezer that we used to store meat, fish, and frozen fruit and vegetables. The news about Mami's passing spread far beyond Whiteland and friends and family members stopped by over a two-week period to pay their respects.

The house was filled with visitors and we fed everyone who came to pay their respects to Mami. Many of Mami's friends and family members stopped by. Her eldest sister Aunty Lena came in their truck from Guaracara. Mami's friends from Whiteland stopped by to spend time with us. The house was teeming with visitors. I visited with my aunts, cousins, and neighbours. I made sure to check in with Daddy when he wasn't inundated with visitors to his bedroom who stopped in to see him and keep his spirits up. Miss Claudia's daughter Nicky, our next-door neighbour, came to sing along with other members of a makeshift band from a church near Monwash. One musician played the djembe drum. Nicky's husband, a part-time youth pastor, played the keyboards and several women sang in three-part harmony.

Before long more and more visitors gathered in our living room, which was standing room only. The singers sang "Fire," a well-known hymn, with the maracas and tambourine playing rhythmically. Mourners began singing in accompaniment and played additional instruments such as the toc toc. They swayed and sang to the solemn but joyous sounds of a Caribbean wake where loved ones are remembered with exuberance for the lives they lived. I made a pot of coffee and offered it to the elderly people who sat politely on the veranda taking in the sounds and visiting with one another. I let the water come to a boil before pouring the brown powder of the instant coffee in. I added a considerable amount of cream and enough sugar to make it sweet, but not distasteful. After a few sips, the mourners kept placing their orders for more. My coffee was a hit and they kept me busy for at least an hour, making and serving, serving and making, in the sweltering Trinidadian heat. Outside, I could hear the voices of inebriated men shouting, laughing, and carrying on over the music. And although we were keeping wake for Mami, my sadness subsided for a short while. Our visitors made me forget why we were there.

The next morning, December 14, 2013, Aunty Linda and Uncle Joseph got into it. As a child, I remember how they fought and nothing had changed after all these years. Uncle Joseph always chose her to iron his shirts for school. She often protested, indicating that it was unfair for him to choose her when other siblings were available as well. Aunty Linda complained about my uncle but I did not witness their entire exchange. I only heard her complaining to Aunty Juliet. When I interjected, Aunty Linda told me to "hush" because I did not know the whole story. As a niece, and much younger than all the other siblings, I needed to know my place and that place was to remain silent when "big people" were talking or when what was being spoken of was none of my business. And after earning advanced degrees in Canada, in Trinidad I am reduced to a child in the presence of my aunts and uncle.

Later that day, when there were no strangers in our house, we heard a public service announcement about the recently deceased in Whiteland. The sound was deafening and came from a small blue car, perhaps a Corolla. The driver sat on the right side and the announcer read the text into a megaphone in careful and measured English and drove through Whiteland repeating the announcement and giving community members the opportunity to record the date of the funeral.

"Funeral arrangements—for Lawrencia "Shoon" Jack—daughter of Benacio and Virginia Garcia...mother of Judy, Marian, Juliet—Gemma, Erroline...grandmother of Anita, Merlynda, Stacey, Dayne—great-grandmother of Jessica, Obidiah, Josiah—beloved sister of Juanita, Lena, Frederick, Marta, Geraldo...." I froze and my heart began to quicken. Mami's passing was real. She was gone. This was the first moment when it really hit me that Mami was no more. The announcement sent everyone in our home into a tailspin. It sent shockwaves through our home. Aunty Erroline, who remained calm and steady up until that point, began crying and moving about erratically. When I heard my name called, I knew that I had to brace myself. I knew that the worst was yet to come.

That night, we were scheduled to have "prayers" as a continuation of the wake. By this point, all of Mami's children had arrived in Trinidad and settled into one of the three houses on our lot. As the night before, the musicians played; however, the tone of the service was more sombre. Everyone was showered and wore nice clothing for the service. Mourners began to fill the living room and sat in chairs or around the dining room table. The veranda was also full of mourners who sat eating and socializing, and other guests milled about in the yard outside. A lay preacher and Mami's friend, Mr. Das, led each hymn and read verses from the Bible. The music was soothing, but the mood made me sad and it felt as though I was in church.

Blessed assurance
Jesus is mine
Oh what a foretaste
Of glory divine
Heir of Salvation
Purchase of God
Born of His spirit
Washed in His blood...

I sat beside Daddy, who lay stretched out on the living room couch. The singers sang with reverence and serenity and in spite of myself, I began to wail. I tried to compose myself, but couldn't. And in a room full of my loved ones, I couldn't catch my breath. No one said or did anything, they simply let me cry as the singers continued their song. Uncle Reagy sat beside me and hugged me, and then he began to cry. I am not sure if my crying had a domino effect. What I do know is that I needed that release. I needed to prepare for the funeral that seemed like eons away.

ALMOST INSTINCTIVELY after Mami's passing, I began to think about my role as a mother to Kennedy. It's as though losing Mami brought motherhood into a crystalized focus for me. I began to think about the fact that Kennedy would not have my mother in her life. I started to mull over how her identity would be developed as having a Black mother and living in Kingston, a predominantly white city. With Mami's passing, I thought about Kennedy as a mixed-race child more intensely. Kennedy was born in 2008. Before her birth, Eric's family members weighed in on what she might look like. Would the baby have my features or his? Would her hair be like mine, inquired my mother-in-law, her voice filled with both caution and apprehension. I did not have all the answers and told myself that only time would tell. Whenever I came across a picture of a mixed-race child in a fashion magazine, I paused and took a good look, forcing myself to see my future child through the eyes of someone else.

I remember one Tommy Hilfiger ad that featured a beautiful little boy. He had olive skin, dark brown hair, and blue eyes. He was "model perfect" with a natural tan and perfectly placed features. His teeth reminded me of Excel chewing gum and I wondered if my baby would look like him. I reminded myself that I needed to be open to the possibility that my child would not look like this child, a fantasy created to sell clothing. I learned that I was more deeply concerned about race and its impact on my family, even though I had not articulated many of those concerns to Mami.

Once, I called home seeking Mami's advice. I was invited to an event at Queen's where the library of Robertson Davies, Eric's great-uncle, was being donated from the personal estate of Robertson's daughter. Before the event, I visited the Queen's employee responsible for organizing the event. And because she was not expecting Robertson to have a Black relative, albeit through marriage, I was met with the racism and exclusion that I had become accustomed to at Queen's and in Kingston. After the encounter, I called Mami asking her whether I should bother attending the event at all. Mami listened to what the encounter was like for me and even though Eric was not scheduled to attend the event, Mami urged that I needed to be there because Eric and I were married and we already had a child together. After speaking with Mami, I always felt as though I needed to remain in Kingston, dedicated to my family, in spite of the racism and the exclusion. Mami always highlighted that I had a responsibility to Kennedy and Eric, despite the personal slights that I experienced as a Black person living in the city.

When I first laid eyes on Kennedy, I felt joy in seeing the little being that grew inside of me for nine months, complete with a voracious appetite and an inability to remain still. I yearned to meet my child and was satisfied when she was finally presented to me. As a newborn, Kennedy had straight, jet black hair and pale skin. Her eyes were a deep blue with hazel flecks showing through in the background. I watched in awe as she was brought near to my face. A large white sheet covered my body from my chest to my toes, cutting me off from the messiness of the birth that lay beneath. It seemed as though time stood still. Kennedy was strangely familiar. With her birth, I also struggled to make sense of issues of race, even though I understood it academically. Eric and I had few answers to questions about Kennedy's racial identity because nothing in our culture prepared us for who she was, the child of a Black mother and a white father. And although my work forced me to think about race on an academic level, I did not have all of the answers on a personal level. For one, Eric did not have the same understanding about issues of race as I did and there were instances where our discussion would break down into a misunderstanding that led to an argument. In some instances, it was easier for me to say nothing about race for fear that it would create another tense moment between us. Speaking about Kennedy and her racial identity became a topic that I could no longer avoid. In having to think through what we would call her, I began to contemplate that she did not fit neatly into constructions of whiteness or Blackness. So much of how I operate in the world is based on race. When I try to erase the concept of race from my mind, I realize before long that my entire world is based on constructions that were not of my making.

Despite my knowing that race is a construction, in my day-to-day interaction in the world I am seen as a Black woman and the world responds to me according to the value that is placed upon Blackness in Canada's racial caste system. With Kennedy's birth, I began to consider how she might experience the world. Would she experience more or less racism than me? Would her light skin shield her from slights that I am often subjected to as a dark-skinned woman? Will her social-class privilege provide a hedge of protection against a Blackness that our culture simply cannot stand?

Kennedy was born at Kingston General Hospital. There were no unusual occurrences at the time of my check-in and although I suffered complications during the birth and had to have an emergency Caesarean section, the overall experience was nothing short of surreal. Although my race did not seem to be an issue for staff at the hospital, Kennedy's birth created what I call a racial stir. My daughter was so fair at birth, white nurses visited our room to see the "Black woman who gave birth to a white baby." Weak from the C-section and exhausted after twelve hours of labour, at first we did not realize that the frequent "visits" to our door had anything to do with race. That was until one nurse admitted why she came. My being a Black woman giving birth to a mixed-race child in a predominantly white city created the stir.

When the nurses arrived to "see," it became clear to me that racial moments arise in my life, even at times when I least expect it. Nurses arriving at the door to see my newborn baby is a racial moment because under normal circumstances, nurses do not visit white newborn babies to have a gander. At the time, I did not know that white curiosity about my mixed-raced child would continue for the rest of her young life. Situated as we were as one of few mixed-raced families in Kingston, the nurses' behaviour must be read as the Othering of racial difference. My Blackness in relation to the supposed whiteness of Kennedy was rendered odd, new, strange, or miraculous. The contrast between my Blackness and my daughter's supposed whiteness was responsible for the stir. It was Kennedy's unexpected whiteness that created the racial surprise and forced nurses who were not assigned to my room to go out of their way to "see."

The myth surrounding the potency of Black genes circulates within our culture to this day. It is the racist myth of the one-drop rule. The "one-drop rule" governed classifications of race in the United States and is a good illustration of this point. It is the idea that one drop of Black "blood" is strong enough to erase whiteness, hence the historical classification of individuals with one drop of Black blood as "Black." Other cultural references speak to this idea of Blackness as "potent" or "strong." For example, as a child I heard, "Once you go Black you never go back" speaking of white-Black interracial unions. It was often discussed in reference to Black men being such good lovers to white women that after dating a Black man once, a white woman will never date a white man again. I raise this point of the supposed potency of Blackness because it explains the "surprise" of Kennedy's alleged whiteness.

This surprise can be read in relation to cultural myths that construct Blackness as eradicating whiteness. In the case of Kennedy's birth, the one-drop rule did not ring true in that racial moment. The nurses saw that a dark-skinned Black woman gave birth to a baby who looked white to them. They came to see Kennedy because my Blackness was supposed to erase my husband's whiteness. I was supposed to give birth to a baby with much darker skin, if we follow this line of thinking. Their surprise by Kennedy's skin colour must be understood against my Black body, especially when my body is read as out of place and unexpected within the context of the hospital and the predominantly white city.

Because white babies are the norm at the hospital, even if Kennedy looked "white" at the time of her birth, her whiteness could not be surprising given that the majority of babies born in the hospital are white. The spectacle surrounding Kennedy's race had as much to do with who we were as an interracial couple and what we were, a couple staying in the Davies Wing, named after Eric's family. Each of these tentacles played a role in how Kennedy was "seen" as opposed to any bona fide racial identity. Put another way, notions about her race could not be separated from who I was as her Black mother and who Eric was as her white father, born to a wealthy Kingston family. My Blackness was the reason why her supposed whiteness needed to be "seen" in the first place. The "miracle" of my giving birth to a "white" baby began by reading my Black body as racial text and the assumptions that surround Blackness in Canadian society.

Race is a difficult construct to unpack and understand. Because "race" can be seen with respect to phenotypic characteristics such as skin colour and eye colour, we are invited to believe that it can be reduced to the level of the biological. When I am in the academy teaching, I discuss that race lacks any biological relevance. Yet, in my everyday life away from the ivory tower, I rarely hear discussions of race that speak to this. In my day-to-day life, the discourse surrounding race is biologically fixed and I am trapped between what I study and what I live, between the academic and the popular.

As a member of a multiracial family, we are often silenced by the weight of popular notions of race by friends, family members, and the general public. Once on a visit to my doctor's office in Kingston, the doctor who saw me at the after-hour clinic commented on how beautiful

Kennedy was and proceeded to inquire, "What does her father look like?" in a thick, South African accent. I remember another instance when we were grocery shopping at Loblaws. An elderly white man who looked like a farmer approached us to take a look at Kennedy. He awe-d and aaah-ed and then asked us who her mother was. When Eric pointed to me, the man remarked, "That's the mother?" with absolutely no sense that his expression of surprise might hurt my feelings. This situation repeated itself often during the first year of Kennedy's life. However, once her hair texture began to change and her brown ringlets began to appear, the attention that our family received morphed from one of surprise to one of admiration for her "beauty."

At a very young age, Kennedy became conscious of her racial identity despite not having the words to describe what she was noticing. At about the age of two, I was watching the Oprah Winfrey show and was surprised when Kennedy walked up to the television and gently caressed Oprah's face while repeating, "Mama, mama…." I was taken aback because I didn't think that Kennedy would notice my skin colour. I was even more surprised that she did not see a difference between the image on the screen and my being in front of her. What she may have been trying to say was, "I see someone else who looks like you." At that point in our lives, we had little interaction with my Trinidadian family. Kennedy did not know Mami and I began feeling badly that she was not being exposed to Trinidadian culture.

Around the time when Kennedy began to create full sentences, she began to inquire about why I was "brown" and why Eric was "pink." I did not have all the answers. How does one explain to a two-year-old a concept that many adults find difficult to grasp? At two, Kennedy understood that she was not quite like me or Eric. In Canadian society, I am invited never to "see" race. This tendency for Canadians to rely on colour blindness instead of delving deeply into the messiness of race speaks to my experiences. To see, witness, and name race in Canada remains taboo, especially for Black people. As a Black Canadian of Trinidadian descent, I am invited to ignore how I experience my life.

Racism is reduced to a mere coincidence or a fluke rather than a tightly organized system with economic consequences for non-white people. If I am ever the victim of racism, I know that I will pay a hefty price for suggesting that it is so. Our culture calls it "playing the race card" when I name race, despite the fact that the race card is always "in play," with all people at all times, even when Black bodies are not present.

When two white men play and strike a business deal, the race card is in play. It is in play because both individuals understand that they are in a racial moment that is devoid of Blackness. This business interaction will be informed by their prior relationship with each other, their social class backgrounds, status in the community, their gender, sexual orientation, and so on. Because both men are white, we are apt to believe that race is not "in play" but it is. *Because* they are both white, race is in play. Race is at the fore in this interaction in the same way that it would inform the exchange if Eric played golf with a Black business associate for the first time. This is a fact of race that few would admit to. It is a fact of race that we are conditioned "not to see" in Canada.

One of my thesis supervisors, Audrey Kobayashi (2000), writes about this in an essay co-authored with Linda Peake called "Racism Out of Place: Thoughts on Whiteness and an Antiracist Geography in the New Millennium." I was introduced to this concept of an antiracist geography as a doctoral student at Queen's. The authors tell us that race is *always* in play, even in the absence of racialized peoples. They suggest that issues of race impact places and spaces, and emphasize that spatial racialization involves placing everyone in "specific, but highly variable, circumstances" (p.395). Place matters because social processes, such as whiteness, rely on specific landscapes and spatial interpretations. An examination of those "empty spaces" where Black bodies are rendered absent, such as the golf course, works to uncover the silence, exclusion, and denial of race and in the process, reinforces whiteness (p.400).

I am invited to believe that the race card is being "played" only when I say that racism impacts my everyday experiences. My Black body becomes the text that the "race card" metaphor needs to make sense. Without my Black body, the idea of the "race card" cannot be true. The metaphor of the game is useful here because I am made to feel that my claims of racial discrimination are never legitimate, but are contrived and manipulated in the same way that players in a card game strategize to make the winning move. I also think about the ways in which being accused of playing the race card becomes a weapon of silence. Being accused of playing the race card is used as a form of ridicule and punishment if I speak out. Silence is used to police what I can and cannot say. Speaking about race remains taboo in Canada because our culture has created the conditions to ensure that I will pay a price for naming it.

One day Kennedy and I were shopping at Winners near the Cataraqui mall when a child asked me whether I was Kennedy's mom. Kennedy stood close to me as I made my way through the large racks of clothing. She was busy playing hide-and-go-seek when a four-year-old who appeared to be a Filipino girl stopped dead in her tracks at the sight of us. With wide eyes, she inquired, "Are you her mommy?" while pointing to Kennedy. When I answered "Yes," she replied in earnest, "...but her skin colour is different." To this remark, I smiled and replied, "Yes, it sure is." Unsatisfied with my answer and understanding that she should not have been carrying on a conversation with a complete stranger, she registered her dissatisfaction with my answer and quickly ran away. This little girl, let's call her Elsa, was brave enough to name what she saw. She saw a mother who looked different from her daughter. In this child's mind, Kennedy could not belong to me because we did not look "the same." Elsa was able to verbalize that which many adults would never dare to do.

Speaking about race remains taboo in Canada precisely because it is deemed rude to openly talk about it. This causes discussions about race to go underground. Open discussion about race is replaced with eye contact in the form of staring. As a multiracial family we were stared at each time we left our home. In staring at my family whenever we were in public, adults who were afraid to ask questions about race for fear of being labelled a "racist," stared instead. The gaze, along with other forms of public surveillance of mixed-race couples, becomes one of the ways in which racial border-crossing and interracial marriage is policed. When Eric and I booked hotel rooms, we were often policed in a way white or Black couples aren't. When we share that we are in fact married, looks of suspicion are replaced by lukewarm acceptance, if at all. The idea is that I am most often assumed to be his prostitute, but never his wife.

WE PLANNED TO have Kennedy. We were desperate to have a child. Eric was on the verge of turning fifty and I sensed that my biological clock was about to sound its last tick-tock. We fantasized about how a child would change our lives. Would we be able to sleep in until 9:00 a.m., making love if we felt like it, ignoring intruding phone calls? Would we be able to travel to exotic countries around the world, only enduring each other's tendencies and faults, thousands of miles away from home? We wanted and needed a child in our lives, despite the fact that her very essence created a complexity surrounding race that neither of us anticipated. At the time, we sensed that we were embarking on several journeys at once, anticipating being first-time parents and, simultaneously, first-time parents to a child that might not look like either of us or members of our respective families. As a Black Canadian woman, I understood that we would face challenges with respect to our interracial marriage and our newborn child; however, I could never have anticipated what those challenges would be.

Eric, who was born into privilege, was only beginning to see race's insidious nature, lurking in the shadows and appearing when we least expected it. Eric's father, Michael, was the owner and publisher of the Kingston Whig Standard, Canada's longest daily newspaper. The paper was in the Davies family for three generations. His great-uncle

Robertson Davies is one of Canada's most beloved authors. When I first met Eric and he told me that Robertson was his uncle, I laughed out loud and told him he was delusional. I shared with Eric that I was an English major at the University of Toronto and that I studied *Fifth Business* during my first year of studies. When he looked at me with serious eyes and I registered that his words were true, my disbelief turned to fear. I did not truly believe that I would be accepted into a family of that stature, more so because of their wealth and also because of my race.

When I called home in excitement and shared the news that I met Eric, Mami listened carefully and was pleased. She told me that she was happy for me. She reminded me that I was "sickly" and warned me never to settle down with a man who would yell or scream at me. She told me that Eric sounded as though he loved me and that I had her blessing, along with Daddy's. When I told her that I was afraid that Eric's family may not accept me because of my race, Mami told me never to worry about that. She explained that if he really loved me, he would protect me and look out for me. Mami told me that marriage itself was not easy, especially in the first five years. She warned me not to be "hasty" and reminded me to keep my temper in check. She asked me about his mother, Elaine, and told me to be nice to everyone, especially my future sisters-in-law. She warned me to always be and dress like a lady and to take care of Eric by putting him first in all things. But Mami could not have understood the many lines that I crossed when our worlds united.

During the first five years of our marriage, Eric couldn't "see" racism. During our engagement, we rarely spoke about race or racism, drunk as we were on romance and a long-distance relationship. I did, however, ask Eric about what my experience would be like if I moved to the city of Kingston and to this, he promised that his friends and family "didn't see colour."

However, racial slights that I experienced, even as we stood holding hands, often went unnoticed. Some of Eric's acquaintances, who had ignored me, or "pretended" not to see me days before when I was alone, would suddenly "recognize" me with grand gestures of "Heeeeellloooooo…" and "How are you?" (kiss-kiss-kiss, hug-hug-hug, fake-fake-fake!) in his presence. Their hypocrisy made my stomach turn. I noticed that my being with Eric offered some protection from the daily microaggressions that life in Kingston became for me. And while I was careful never to rely on it, I often used the opportunity to observe the behaviour of others. I became a student of race. I used the opportunity to act as a researcher of sorts, tasked with writing the dissertation of our lives.

With Kennedy's birth, issues of race took up permanent residence in our home like an unwanted house guest who refuses to leave. Although Eric and I were deliberate in marrying each other, neither of us were prepared for the cruelty of our choice to start a family, first by the wider culture and then by some family members, friends, and acquaintances. On the one hand, I understood that race is a fabrication and the creation of the ruling elite with the power to make the "rules." I understood that race changes over periods of time and within specific geographic regions. At one time Jews were not considered white, neither were Italians or the Irish.

In my everyday life I experience race as a real "thing." To some, it is a monster that ravages the psyche, creating sickness, mental illness, and nervous breakdowns. Yet, there is little discussion of the legacy of slavery and the transatlantic slave trade on the lives of Black people and Black families in particular. Racism attacks our self-esteem, inviting us to believe that there is little pride in being Black. We call it internalized racism. We internalize negative images and ideas about who we are and of our capabilities. The good news is that I am from a resilient people. My ancestors were wise and strong. Racism brings about pain. It is the pain of knowing that in Canada, I am often reminded that there is something wrong with Blackness. At times the concept of race is difficult for me to accept because I was born into a race-based hierarchy that I have no control over. On a daily basis, racism is senseless and confusing because I am punished for a skin colour that I did not choose.

As a mixed-race family, we must continually make sense of our relationships with family, friends, and acquaintances. We must also interact with institutions such as schools, churches, the legal system, the medical system, law enforcement, and private industry in ways that are often different from same-race families. My choosing to write about our experiences as a mixed-race family puts me at risk of being castigated, shunned, and ostracized. But I write so that I can help other families who are embarking on the journey that my family took. And if I can support even one person with my words, I will be satisfied.

Track 6:
ODE TO GUERLAIN

Soundtrack:

Let It Be
The Beatles

Bohemian Rhapsody
Queen

I Still Haven't Found What I'm Looking For
U2

Kind of Blue
Miles Davis

El Diablo Suerte
Daisy Voisin

A La Media Noche
Daisy Voisin

Bahia Girl
David Rudder

War
Bob Marley & the Wailers

Sweet Soca Man
Baron

AUNTY JULIET AND I travelled all over San Fernando, it seemed, as we made preparations for the funeral. We visited the Registrar's Office to pick up Mami's death certificate. We went to a bakery and ordered batches of fresh kaisers. As we drove, Aunty Juliet's phone rang incessantly. "Yes, we in San Fernando...give it to Marian next door... we comin' up home just now." And so it went, all day long. Later, we picked up Aunty Marian and went to the funeral home to choose the casket. The main room felt quiet. There were no windows and I was claustrophobic. It was difficult to breathe. There were several caskets on display. There was a white one that was much too narrow and a black casket I knew Mami would not like. Aunty Marian and I stopped near a mahogany casket with a rich beige interior. We looked at each other and almost simultaneously agreed that we found the one. Aunty Juliet advised the sales clerk that we were interested in purchasing it and was quickly whisked away to complete the sale. I joined them, leaving Aunty Marian for a moment. I sat at the desk and pulled out two lipsticks from my purse. I told Aunty Juliet that I wanted the lipsticks to be buried with Mami. The brown lipstick in the silver tube was to be placed inside the casket to symbolize eternity. I explained carefully that the red lipstick in the black tube, Au Chaud, was to be applied to her lips, because it was her favourite colour. I was clear that only the lipstick in the silver tube, which seemed to be made of a tin-like material, was to remain in the casket to be buried so it would be with her forever.

Aunty Juliet looked nervous and cautioned me that the mortician might get the two colours mixed up. Frustrated, I told Aunty Juliet that Au Chaud, the red lipstick, was the obvious choice for Mami's skin colour and that the morticians would not make such a mistake. She acquiesced reluctantly and asked the associate to include the instructions for the red lipstick to be applied to Mami's lips and for the silver tube to remain in the casket for the burial.

After leaving the funeral home, we stopped for lunch at a Chinese restaurant in San Fernando named Aquarium. We were seated promptly. Aunty Marian was in great spirits. She was bubbly and funny as usual. She ordered beef fried rice. Aunty Juliet opted for the roasted pork with lo mein and I ordered the satay chicken on white rice with mixed vegetables. To drink we ordered three shandy Caribs in ginger, sorrel, and lime and three glasses of cold flat water.

When we arrived home that afternoon, I visited Daddy in his room. He asked me where I was. That was code for, "You haven't been visiting me enough." Normally, on my trips home, I spent each morning talking with Daddy and brought him up to speed on my life in Canada. I filled him in on my teaching at Queen's, my in-laws, Kennedy and her schooling, and so on. But on this trip, I hardly had the time to visit with him given that there were so many preparations to make. I told Daddy about my day in San Fernando and about all the places we went. He lay on his tummy, as was his custom, with his hands underneath his pillow and his face turned to one side allowing him to speak. He asked me what time it was and when I said that it was close to 6:00 p.m. he remarked, "What is this...time flying," and asked me to tell Aunty Juanita that he was ready for his tea. And in that moment, I could see that he was missing Mami. They were married for sixty years. I wondered what it must have felt like to lose a spouse after six decades together. But I didn't know how to console him. I saw that he was lonely but I couldn't bring her back. And as much as I wanted to console him in that moment I didn't want to cry, and instead tried to keep our interaction as light as possible.

THE NEXT MORNING, Aunty Juliet reminded me that she, Uncle Wayne, Uncle Joseph, and I would be visiting Mami at the morgue for a viewing later that night at 7:00 p.m. I was petrified. I didn't know what to expect and had never been to a morgue before. Speaking with Uncle Joseph, I shared with him that I had changed my mind about going and that I was too nervous to attend. He encouraged me to face my fear and reminded me that because Eric is ten years older than I am, funerals would become customary for us as his friends and family members begin to pass on. But I felt like cancelling. I felt like backing out and considered that perhaps I should wait until the funeral to see her. I couldn't shake the feeling the entire day and tried to keep myself busy.

Although I lost my nerve, I simply could not let Aunty Juliet go to the viewing on her own. I knew she needed my support and seeing the merits of Uncle Joseph's argument, I made up my mind and resolved to be strong. But throughout the day, I felt as though Mami was compelling me to visit her, to see her. I felt a strong pulling. It's as though the only thing I could concentrate on was seeing her. The feeling was so strong that I couldn't ignore it. The urging felt like the presence of a constant reminder that I had to see her beforehand rather than wait for the funeral. The urging developed into a knowing that I could not ignore throughout the day and nothing made the urgency of that pull towards Mami go away. The strong urge towards the funeral home did not make sense to me at the time and I did not share my feelings with anyone.

That evening, we travelled in a white Honda Civic along Poonah Road towards San Fernando. When we arrived at the funeral home, I opened the door cautiously. We were ushered into a small room where Mami's body lay. I was not prepared to see her in the casket. She looked beautiful in her blue lace dress. Everything looked perfect, except for her lipstick! The mortician applied the brown lipstick instead of Au Chaud and my heart sank and then I knew instinctively that I was being called to fix the mistake. I protested straight away.

Can someone please make sure…
That my Mami's lipstick is changed to the red one instead of the brown!
How could this mistake happen?
We told you to apply the red and not the brown colour…
Can you please reassure us that by tomorrow the proper colour will be applied?…

I was frustrated and felt like crying. I was upset and held back tears of fury. Aunty Juliet scolded me. She reminded me that she knew all along that the wrong lipstick would be applied, and I was crushed. Exhausted, I left she, Uncle Wayne, and Uncle Joseph in the viewing area and took a seat near the door of the funeral parlour. I watched as people walked by in the dim light of dusk as Aunty Juliet made last-minute arrangements with the staff. My heart was heavy. We left the funeral parlour and I hoped and prayed that the red lipstick would be applied in time for the funeral. I knew that I owed it to Mami.

We made our way back to the car. Soca music played as we drove through the busy streets of San Fernando, past Marabella and then through Gasparillo on the way home. From the car speakers we could hear "Sweet Soca Man" by Baron from a CD my cousin Damian made for Uncle Wayne. I listened quietly as Aunty Juliet outlined what we were to expect the next day. And in the stillness of the backseat, I thought about the funeral and about Mami coming to our house the next morning. I thought about being drawn to the funeral home so strongly and reminded myself to always pay attention to my intuition as my guide and compass. The strong feeling began to subside and I understood in that moment that my relationship with Mami extended beyond death. Not even her passing could destroy the bond between us. I took comfort in the realization that death is not the end and that there was something more to Mami's passing that I needed to pay attention to. I realized in that moment that even with Mami gone, I had access to her in a different realm and that gave me some comfort. I knew that her passing was not the end and that I had to pay close attention to the ways that Mami would still remain part of my life.

Track 7:
CALL OF THE MANDOLIN

Soundtrack:

Sereno Sereno
Daisy Voisin

I Can't Make You Love Me
Bonnie Raitt

Demons
Imagine Dragons

Lord Watch Over Our Shoulders
Garnett Silk

If Tomorrow Never Comes
Garth Brooks

A Change Is Gonna Come
Sam Cooke

Jesus, Take the Wheel
Carrie Underwood

Good Mother
Jann Arden

Angel from Montgomery
Bonnie Raitt

Aᴼᴛᴇʀ ʀᴇᴛᴜʀɴɪɴɢ from the funeral home, I could not sleep. That night, I tossed and turned and tried my best to settle my mind. Lying beside Aunty Linda, I felt her breathing gently and steadily. On Poonah Road, the cars whizzed by in the wee hours of the morning, the music blared loudly from base-ridden speakers and faded away as they left our village. Out in the yard, the dogs howled and fought each other. At one point, I left the warmth of my bed and headed over to the window to see what the commotion was all about. Sticking my head out of the window, I could barely see a beige-coloured dog who appeared to be digging a hole at the corner of Mami's garden, right near where the concrete began. I headed back to bed and saw one hour pass to the next on the alarm clock. Soon enough, night turned to day and morning came.

At daybreak, our family was in a frenzy. Our house was tense in anticipation of Mami's body arriving. We made arrangements for her body to come to the house, as well as to arrive at the church, so that Daddy could say his final goodbye. Unable to see from glaucoma, Daddy took few trips outside our home, except for visits to the doctor or to Easter Sunday lunch at Aunty Juliet's house in San Fernando. My tummy felt hollow. I was nervous. I felt like throwing up and as though I was preparing to give a speech to an unknown audience that I was unprepared for.

Aunty Marian, Aunty Juliet, and Aunty Juanita were busy in the kitchen, preparing food for mourners who returned to our house after the ceremony. We wore our Sunday best...black dresses, black suits, leather handbags, and red lipstick. I was not entirely sure about the exact time the body would arrive, but from the increase in energy and commotion inside the house, I knew when it came. From the back hallway of our house, I could see the mahogany casket being removed from the back of the hearse.

My heart quickened and it was difficult to breathe. In my high-heeled stilettos, I paced back and forth in the living room. It was hard for me to be still, knowing that the casket was being erected on a large stand at the front of the house, near Mami's garden. The stand was provided by the funeral home and the men, Uncle Joseph, Uncle Wayne, and Uncle Reagy helped secure the casket in place. A tent was raised, and rows of white plastic chairs were arranged in a "U" shape. Mami's body lay peacefully in the middle for easy viewing. In an instant, I heard Aunty Juanita screaming outside. She had gone to see the body and needed to make peace with Mami's passing. She wept loudly telling everyone that Mami had asked her to visit, but that she was too busy and didn't make it. It was gut-wrenching to listen to her cry of regret and remorse for a favourite sister who left her so suddenly.

I made my way to the front porch and approached the open casket. A prayer, Psalm 23: The Lord is My Shepherd, was written on a poster strewn with pink orchids near Mami's face. Through the haunting wails of Aunty Juanita, my legs began feeling weak. Uncle Joseph, a part-time lay pastor in England, shouted prayers of comfort. Husbands held wives too fragile to stand.

Soon, Aunty Juliet led Daddy towards the coffin. He was dressed in his Sunday best, wearing a white guayabera shirt with grey slacks and leather Caribbean slippers. He wore his favourite fedora, a grey hat with soft feathers at the side. Aunty Juliet led Daddy carefully by his right arm and he searched the air with his left, until he was told that he was near the coffin. Aunty Juliet sat him on a chair beside Mami's head. Looking up to the sky, he reached down and caressed Mami's face. With his fingers he carefully felt her cheeks, her nose, and her mouth, as if to confirm that this really was his wife of sixty years. I wondered for a moment what Mami felt like, knowing that I did not have the guts to caress her in that way. Did she feel cold, like ice, I wondered? But Daddy did not cry. He touched her face until he was satisfied. I wondered how Daddy was able to keep his composure, bury a woman that he loved so tenderly for all those years. Aunty Juliet led him quietly back to his bedroom. Seeing Daddy say his final goodbye to Mami gave me the courage I needed.

As Daddy was being led back to his bedroom, I finally mustered the nerve to walk near where her body lay. Uncle Joseph had urged us to speak and to "let it out." I remember hearing myself thanking her for being my mother. I remember thanking her for taking care of me. And I remember screaming out to the heavens, "Jesus!", "Jesus!", "Jesus!" with the same guttering wail of the pig that Daddy and his friends killed when I was a child. I knew I did not have another chance to thank her, but my body betrayed me. I wanted to stand tall. I wanted to speak with dignity and respect, but my knees gave way. I remember that Uncle Wayne held me, preventing me from falling on the hard, uneven concrete. I remember being put on a chair beside the coffin and being fanned, my feet numb and lifeless.

From the comfort of my chair, I looked at Mami's face. I really looked at her. I saw that Au Chaud had been applied. Through my tears, my heart danced because Mami looked her best. She looked like herself with the red lipstick she was known for. I was proud of her. Mami was as beautiful as she always was. Forcing myself to take deep breaths, my hysteria gave way to gentle sobbing. In the chair, sitting next to her body, I remained a child fully aware that the person who I loved the most was no more.

Mami's body remained at the house for approximately one hour. Neighbours visited from both near and far. Aunty Juliet made arrangements for taxis to take us to Mayo Roman Catholic. The church was simple and when we arrived, the musicians who played for us at the wake two nights before were in attendance. They sang Mami's favourite hymns and the casket was wheeled towards the centre of the aisle near the altar. I wrote one of the eulogies that was read; however, we decided that my cousin Maurice would read it on behalf of all the grandchildren and great-grandchildren. I sat in the front row at the right side of the aisle. Behind me, but at the end of the aisle, my cousin Quanicy was distraught and screamed and sobbed uncontrollably.

Mami had asked Quanicy to visit her before her passing, but Quanicy got tied up with her studies. She was taking a course as a dental hygienist and was distraught because Mami paid for the course from her savings. Years before when our house burned down, Quanicy, her brother Quaton, and her mother, my Aunt Gemma, were living with Mami and Daddy. She spent so much time with Mami as a child that she had also developed a strong bond with her. But it wasn't only Quanicy who was in a state. All of Mami's grandchildren were deeply impacted by her passing. Each of us had a special bond to Mami because she demonstrated her love for us and we knew that we could rely on her for comfort.

After a short service led by Mr. Das, we began to file out of the church. It was standing room only. Aunty Marian fainted near Mami's coffin as the pallbearers attempted to move the casket from the church to the hearse that waited on the street outside. Tears streaming down her face and wailing beyond comprehension, the men tried to lift Aunty Marian to her feet, her body stretched lifeless on the ground in the middle of the aisle and dirt soiling her beautiful velvet dress. It was bedlam. It was chaos. The Ides of March was near.

The men impatiently tried to move Aunty Marian's lifeless body out of the way in preparation for Lawrencia's last parang, which was only moments away and to be performed at the grave. Looking behind me from the backseat of the Maxi Taxi that drove along the hillside to the gravesite, I saw a caravan of cars that moved like ants as far as my eyes could see. We arrived at the grave within minutes, the hearse crawling behind.

At the gravesite, perched up on a small hill about 200 metres from our home, friends and family members arrived to witness the burial. Aunty Germine screamed the loudest, causing a scene. She shouted and spoke at the same time, with no tears in her eyes. The youngest sibling loudly asked Mami why she left her so soon. Aunty Germine stood dangerously close to the edge of the grave as she continued her charade.

Whether it was genuine or not, I couldn't really tell. Aunty Juliet chided her and cautioned, "Watch your step before we have another funeral on our hands."

Beneath my sorrow, I saw the humour in the spectacle that she made. The mahogany coffin was lowered into the soft, clay-coloured earth after much manoeuvring by the two gravediggers. The sand was so soft, large swifts of dirt slid into the grave while the men used thick ropes to try to move the coffin squarely into place. The gravediggers began lowering the coffin and within seconds, Mami was resting six feet under the ground. Soon, they began throwing sand on the coffin, taking my breath away. And the voices between my ears made a cacophony of sounds, yelling and carrying on, but no one heard or could save me from my despair.

Wait...no...don't lower the coffin!
Wait...Jesus, please don't put my Mami in the ground...
Wa---it! Someone help! Help me...please.
They're throwing sand on my Mami.
The sand is suffocating my Mami. You're killing my Mami.
She's telling me that she can't breathe.
Can't you hear her?
The sand is covering her up.
My Mami can't breathe...
Someone please, please help me. Can't you see?
My Mami can't breathe...

But no one heard me. Everyone stood motionless, politely sobbing, wiping tears with Kleenex or triangular shaped hankies drenched in Guerlain's Shalimar. I stood alone at the grave without Eric or Kennedy. I left Kennedy with Eric's sister Jennifer and he was scheduled to join me towards the end of my trip, to accompany me back to Kingston. Within moments, we stabbed white carnations into the mound of dirt that looked like the bread that Mami used to bake. The freshly decorated grave was littered with bouquets filled with lily of the valley and orchids. By now the voices between my ears settled, their lungs burnt from sheer exhaustion.

A few yards away, the parang band played Mami's favourite song under an old stone gazebo. "Sereno sereno, sereno, sera, estos son seronos, de la madruga." Uncle Richard, a family friend and former neighbour known for his playing of the cuatro, strummed violently. Uncle Frederick, Mami's brother from New York, shook the chac chac with fervour. Mourners who were able to sing joined in with the chorus. The sound of the mandolin, distinct, loud, and clear, reminded our village that the veil was torn. Mami had already made her transition to another life and her last parang was our chance to say our final goodbye.

I took a rose from Aunty Juliet's hand by its hard, bumpy stem and stuck it into a clear spot on the mound. And although I was deeply saddened, I was satisfied. In the background, the parang band continued to play, forcing us to release our sorrows. I was satisfied that I was there to make peace with losing Mami once again, the funeral acting as a rite of passage that I had to experience in order to make sense of her life and mine.

RETURNING TO THE HOUSE after the funeral, I was spent. I had nothing left in me. Our house was filled with mourners who ate, drank, and helped our family with the heaviness of our hearts that day. The members of the parang band also joined us, had lunch, and continued to play. I picked up the chac chac and joined them. Mourners were mesmerized by my abilities. Perhaps it was the fact that I was a girl playing chac chac so well. Perhaps it was because I was "Canadian." I loved playing the chac chac with memories of Daddy playing in our house and Mami singing along as we fêted into the night. The next day, I slept on the couch in our living room for most of the day, too weary to do much of anything else. I tried to read, but could not make it beyond a few sentences at a time. For some reason, I attempted to get through Patricia Hill Collins's *Black Feminist Thought* in preparation for the class that I was scheduled to teach in January 2014. Looking back, I needed to rest. I needed to heal, but the immediacy of my teaching weighed heavily on my mind.

After the burial, I thought about the fact that Mami was gone, but that my biological mother was still alive. It also occurred to me that Mami's funeral was not the first time that I said goodbye to her. At eleven years old, I was forced to return to Canada to live with my biological mother and I was not prepared. I was about to write the island-wide Common Entrance exam as a Standard Five student at Vos Government School in Gasparillo.

The exam determined whether I would attend a five-year academic or three-year vocation school. Our teachers explained that we needed to bring our identification to school on the morning of the exam. That morning, when my teacher stood beside my desk, at first I thought that he was looking at the answers I wrote on the page. Cautiously, he picked up my Canadian passport that lay to the left of my exam and reported me to the principal.

I was not a Trinidadian citizen and had overstayed my visit in the country, Aunty Juliet was told by the authorities later that week. Mami and Daddy failed to file the legal paperwork authorizing me to stay with them since I was never legally adopted. Within days, I was ordered to leave the island to return to Canada, but it was not Mami or Daddy's wish for me to leave. At that time, I knew that I would eventually have to come back home to Canada to live with my biological mother at some point, but I wasn't ready. I knew that I had to start a new life with her, but I wasn't ready. And when the day came for me to leave Mami and Daddy, dread swept over me. It all happened quite quickly.

I was told years later that when I returned to Canada, Mami became sick with grief. What she didn't know was I was heartbroken. I felt abandoned. I felt betrayed even though they wanted me to stay. I was ripped from the mother who raised me and sent to live with the mother who gave birth to me, based on a technicality. I heard Daddy saying that it was the right thing to do, but I was devastated. And although I was not angry at Mami and Daddy for the separation, I simply never got over it.

Track 8:
THE AFRICAN DUTCHPOT

<u>Soundtrack</u>:

El Nacimiento
Daisy Voisin

Have You Ever Seen the Rain?
Creedence Clearwater Revival

Midnight in Harlem
Tadeschi Trucks Band

Who the Cap Fit
Bob Marley & the Wailers

Murderer
Barrington Levy

Bahia Girl
David Rudder

They Gonna Talk
Beres Hammond

WHEN I RETURNED to Canada after living most of my childhood in Trinidad, the first year was the most difficult. I had to adjust to life without Mami. I wrote her letters because telephone calls were extremely expensive. I went weeks without hearing her voice. At school, I was teased about my dark skin. I am ashamed to admit how much that teasing remains with me today. Words are powerful. When uttered with the intent to wound, they cripple and maim.

"Hey you, you African Dutch pot, African Dutch pot, African Dutch pot! You are so Black, you look like an African Dutch pot!" A freckle-faced boy with squinty eyes, whose name was either Shawn or Shane, I cannot remember now, spat the words at me with all his might, using a cocktail of mockery and scorn. I stood on the concrete school yard that surrounded St. Andrew Catholic School in Toronto's north end. I had just come back to Canada for good that summer. But I missed Mami terribly. Although she always made it a habit of telling me that she loved me, I could tell that she did by the way that she looked at me. Her hazel eyes searched for the almond-coloured panes of my soul and once inside, I knew that I was safe.

Mami was affectionate. Sometimes it was a caress of my face. Sometimes it was the wink of an eye. Sometimes, it was her laughter at me showing her the latest dance craze that she found amusing. I especially enjoyed milling around the kitchen when she cooked, her pot luring us closer to the smells. While she cooked, I often took the dishcloth from the kitchen sink and wiped down the fridge, which was littered with plastic pineapples, bananas, and oranges. When cooking her famous stewed chicken, Mami always called me to give me a taste. She blew the hot stew that she scooped out of the pot so that it wouldn't scorch my hand, and carefully poured it into my palm. Mami was such a good cook that the food always tasted perfect me to. But being her taste-tester made me feel special. Mami always found ways to show me that I meant so much to her. Once she made me say grace for Easter dinner, and I remembered to thank God for her and her cooking. She didn't have to, but she took the time to show that my life made a difference to her.

Mami's laugh was always from the gut, from the heart, and that is where we connected. Mami's love for me wasn't technical and never forced. When I arrived home from school each day, I looked forward to kissing her and greeting her "Good afternoon" as is our custom in Trinidad. When I kissed and hugged her, she smelt like love...warm, soft, safe.

"Shawn"teased me incessantly for what seemed like eons.Accompanying him in his bullying was Wayne. Wayne was also Black, but of Jamaican heritage.Wayne laughed and laughed, and chimed in, "Yeah, you African Dutch pot!" even though he was not much lighter than me.Wayne had perfect teeth and gigantic brown eyes that popped out of his hazelnut-coloured face. And with their taunts, they began to hunt me down like wolves on the attack. They decided, in their wisdom, to trip vulnerable girls. Smaller than most girls in my class and with no friends to call my own, I was an easy target, vulnerable and available, compared to those who played in snowsuited trios and quartets all over the school yard.

Knowing what they were up to, I began to run, but I could not match their speed, nor their strength. In seconds they caught up with me and with one swift kick to my left calf, I fell and landed in the soft, powdery snow. Shawn and Wayne roared with laughter as they kicked the icy powder onto my body.They topped this off with a ritual smearing of a perfectly made snowball into my nose. I fought back with flailing arms and legs, humiliated.

"Stop it! Stop it, stop it or I'm going to tell Ms. Mady on you, you stupid idiots!" But they ignored my cries in haughty, testosteroned triumph and ran away in search of their next target. Feeling dejected and not knowing what to make of their attack, I slowly looked to my left and right. I saw children who were too busy playing tag to notice our "exchange." And even though I felt like crying, I held back my tears.

I stood up and dusted the snow off my face, hair, and the blue "man-on-the-moon" snowsuit that I despised. After recess when I returned to the warmth of the classroom, the sting of the snow on my face slowly dissipated as we settled down to work in the open area. The warmth of the room slowly eased the burn of my cheeks, but I did not utter a word to Ms. Mady. I didn't know where to begin. I was too ashamed to even repeat the awful phrase to her because she herself was white, and although kind, I secretly wondered if she too would laugh at me. By repeating those awful words, I would have to admit that they were directed at me. They were meant for me to believe in their power. And I could not bring myself to do it, even in my own defence, so I chose to suffer in silence.

That experience marked the very first time in my life when someone other than a family member brought my skin colour to the surface. I was surprised by the boys' articulation of the negativity associated with my dark skin because they were strangers. Up until that point, it seemed as though only close relatives spoke in this way. As a child, I remember hearing jokes and comments about skin colour: "Black like tar...," "Black until you're blue...," and "Black like a cobo (vulture)."

Whiteness and being light-skinned was revered by my entire extended family and by the wider culture of the island. The legacy of colonialism created a culture where skin colour is linked to social class and status. Because Papa was born in Venezuela, members of my family clung to the culture that he passed on. Even though we are Afro Trinidadian, growing up I was not exposed to any aspects of a genuine African identity. My identity, and that of my family members, revolved around being Trini, "respectably well off," and being of Venezuelan descent. I had grown accustomed to hearing, "When you're Black, you're in the back, when you're brown you stick around, but when you're white, you're quite alright!"

As a child, I could not conceive of the extent to which whiteness is worshipped globally, nor could I see myself grappling to find a safe space for myself within this idolatry. The question that I am trying to interrogate is whether I can ever truly rid myself of the vestiges of internalized racism, something that many cultures in Canada, including Asian and South Asian communities, also grapple with. I do not feel comfortable talking about internalized racism with my family. Colourism and shadeism will never be erased from my culture, thanks to transatlantic slavery and the legacy of racism that continues to haunt us. Now I must think about Kennedy. I must think about the messages she will receive from the world about her skin colour...about mine. I think about my role in making sure that she does not see dark skin as being suspect, ugly, or bad. What an unfair and uphill battle for me to climb. As it were, she already knows what the world thinks. All she has to do is access TikTok, YouTube, Instagram, cartoons, and popular media.

F RIENDS AND ACQUAINTANCES did not understand me when I told them that I lost my mother. My grief for Mami was often met with indifference or silence. I couldn't understand the cruelty of it all. I wondered how it was that they couldn't see my pain in losing my mother. An academic mentor and colleague, Dr. Kitossa, whose relatives are from Jamaica, emailed me and encouraged me to take care of myself upon hearing the news of Mami's passing. In his email, he said that he understood the close bond that grandparents in the Caribbean often forge with grandchildren, and for the first time since Mami's passing, I felt heard. I hung onto his words knowing that I didn't have to explain how I was feeling.

My being raised by Mami, rather than my biological mother, is soaked in the duality of happiness and pain, acceptance and rejection, and belonging and estrangement. It is a curious place to be. I am both family and an orphan, blood and water. Today, with Mami gone, I am both granddaughter and daughter, sister and niece, to the rest of my family. Living in this space has enabled me to shift seamlessly across familial boundaries and in the process, has opened up new possibilities for other family members who mirrored the model that was established with my rearing.

I look back on my childhood with fondness and gratitude and I am not a victim, even though there have been extremely difficult moments in my life. Mami loved me. She spoke softly to me. She looked at me. She really looked at me. She chided me and scolded me when I needed it. She told me that I was everything and could be anything. When I was with Mami I knew that she would give her life for me. I can't put the bond that we shared into words. When we were together, there was an unspoken tenderness there that I have not felt with anyone else. I would often look at her and knew that she understood how I was feeling at the time.

SOON AFTER I MARRIED ERIC, I began experiencing something that I call "Black liberal guilt." For some reason, Mami's passing brought this concept into sharper focus because after her funeral, I began to reevaluate my life, my marriage, motherhood, and my living in Kingston.

I define Black liberal guilt as the guilt that I feel about my personal success as a Black woman when compared to members of my family or other members of the Black community. It is a type of guilt that makes me wonder whether I should be enjoying the finer things in life. Should I really be dining at this fancy restaurant? Should I be taking a ride on my father-in-law's Hinckley yacht? Should I be spending money on yet another holiday or wear nice clothing when members of my community continue to suffer? In Canadian society, we have not yet created a term for such feelings. Black liberal guilt invites me to believe that I should not enjoy what I have, even though I have worked hard to achieve it.

I once heard a quote from Sammy Davis Jr. I was watching his biography on the Biography Channel and he said that there was no racism like that which a rich, Black man experiences. As a Black woman living in privilege, I am stuck between the surprise, jealousy, and resentment of whites and the resentment, jealousy, and surprise of Black people, topped off by the accusation of "sellout" for marrying a white man. As a culture, we have not yet created the spaces for Black people to be economically privileged. We have not developed the language to speak about the complexities inherent in living between an expectation of Black poverty compared with the reality of Black success.

To illustrate this point, Eric and I attended a fundraiser in Toronto that was hosted by one of his former classmates at Trinity College School. All of his male siblings and his forefathers have attended the school for generations now. His friend's family owned a car dealership in Calgary and were attempting to raise millions of dollars for Toronto's Hospital for Sick Children that year. Eric and I were invited as his special guests. They hired Jennifer Hudson to sing that night and I personally met her and took pictures with her and her family.

On our way into the venue, Eric and I walked hand in hand, dressed as we were in black-tie attire. However, outside the venue, near the photographers and the step-and-repeat was a Black gospel choir. When I saw the choir, my heart sank and I whispered to Eric, "I can't believe they hired a gospel choir for heaven's sake!"

As we walked towards the young girls and boys singing for our pleasure, my Black liberal guilt was activated. I did not want them to see me. I wanted to be invisible. I was wearing a black lace dress and my hair had been recently blown out by Zac from Jazma Hair Salon in Toronto. I did not want them to see me because in seeing me, they would know that I was privileged enough to be invited to the event. I felt guilty. Seeing me entering the building as an invited guest, the gap between who I was as privileged and who they were as a hired choir, was even more emphasized. I did not want them to see me because they gave me that look of confused curiosity that members of my community sometimes register with me, a look that makes me feel trapped between two worlds.

I squeezed Eric's hand and said hello to them as we walked by. That night, I may have been the only Black person at the event, save for the entertainment. Walking past the choir, which represented tokenistic inclusion, made me feel guilty. I knew that they saw me as a Black woman married to a white man. And while I did not feel ashamed or embarrassed to be attending the event, I felt guilty that they were invited to entertain me and that they sang on the outside of the venue, while I was permitted to be on the inside. This time, I wasn't the coat-check girl. I was an invited guest. Geographically, the line between insider and outsider was drawn and I found myself being included. Eric and I enjoyed ourselves that night, but the image of the choir has never left me.

Track 9:
THE WASTELAND

Soundtrack:

The Monster
Eminem ft. Rihanna

Fancy
Iggy Azalea

Fight the Power
Public Enemy

Buffalo Soldier
Bob Marley & the Wailers

This Is a Move
Brandon Lake & Tasha Cobbs Leonard

The Sound of Silence
Simon & Garfunkel

Bridge Over Troubled Water
Simon & Garfunkel

BY THE END OF JANUARY 2014, I knew something was wrong. I fell into a deep depression for the first time in my life. I couldn't sleep at night and lay awake thinking about Mami. I asked myself where she was. I wondered what heaven must be like. I began thinking about her burial and the image of the gravediggers covering the casket with sand played over and over again in my mind's eye. The hairs on my arms felt as though they were perpetually raised.

A crippling fear came over me. I needed to sleep with the lights on for the first time since I was a child. My fear prevented me from entering certain rooms in our home, such as my office, the gym, and part of our unfinished basement. I needed to find a place to write. A writer needs a place of her own. Mami's picture was perched on the back wall of my office, facing my back. I could not bear to see her face, knowing that she was gone. Once when we visited our cottage in the 1000 Islands, New York, for an impromptu overnight stay, I was so crippled by fear we were forced to leave. I needed Eric more than ever. I needed him to accompany me to certain parts of our home or to fetch something from a room that I could not enter. I could not relax when he drove, terrified that we would get into a car accident. And although he was patient, he could not make sense of the changes that I was going through. When I least expected it, I had memories of Mami that would move me to tears. The strangest part was that I began to worry that Mami might follow me around the house or that I might bump into her in my closet or the dining room. I booked a visit with my doctor.

When I admitted to her that I was afraid that Mami was following me, she looked at me as though she had seen a ghost. She began writing furiously on her notepad and observed me with careful eyes.

You are suffering from something called episodic depression...
It is related to your grandmother's death...

Here is a prescription for…
Take one pill each day to get you through the next couple of weeks.
Have you suffered from depression before?…
Doctor's orders…I don't want you by yourself in your home…
Leave the house for at least thirty minutes to one hour each day…
You are not allowed to be alone during this time.
Here is a letter to take to work…
I need you to take a few weeks off from teaching at Queen's…

As she spoke, tears streamed from my eyes. That night, I began taking the pills, even though I try to avoid taking prescription drugs at all cost. I took the pills three days in a row, then flushed the rest down the toilet. I told myself that I couldn't be Black and depressed at the same time. That is simply too much of a burden for me to carry in this world. It did not help that I was already suspicious of doctors who routinely sterilized Black women or who ignored Black patients in a way that they would never ignore white women.

I told myself that I would follow the rest of my doctor's orders to the tee. I left home each day as directed. I filed the doctor's note in one of my hanging folders, ensuring that it would not be seen by our housekeeper. I did not speak to my department head at Queen's about needing time off either, because academic administrators cannot be trusted with private information.

In order to cope, I gave my two weeks' notice at a part-time job that I held at the Kingston Community Health Centre. I did not give a reason except to say that I knew I was on the wrong track career-wise. In truth, I was unable to juggle more than teaching. Living without Mami made me feel desperate. I felt lost and unable to make sense of my life. Teaching was excruciating. I struggled with it for the first time in my career. I am a born teacher. I love teaching, but in the right circumstances. Typically, I look forward to being with students in the classroom, but I found the students exhausting; their constant inquiries into the smallest things wore me down.

One day at the start of winter term 2014, I made my way to class. The students huddled in packs along the stark, dimly-lit hallway, talking and laughing. I barely made my way past their protruding backpacks, their voices making a myriad of sounds about drinking escapades the night before. I once stood where they stood, naïve to the actual realities of teaching. I was hopeful and optimistic. I wanted to "save the world." That was years ago, before I became a "sometimes" professor. That day, I entered the classroom to find garbage on the desk and scrunched up papers that did not make it to the garbage can, along with throw-away pens and pencils that the students left behind. The chalk dust was so thick, I was afraid to lay my students' essays down. At the beginning of the year, I introduced myself to the professor who taught the class before mine. His name was Kyle and he was friendly at first. With time, he became cold and aloof each time I entered the room. He reminded me of the professor, Dr. Matthews, who taught a class next door to mine at the same day and time each week.

Dr. Matthews visited my classroom while I was teaching and urged me to "keep the noise down." His voice was stern and authoritative and his eyes lacked amusement. His chemistry students (read: the "hard sciences") were trying to concentrate on a test and my students (read: "easy-peasy" gender studies stuff) were making it hard for them to think. He chided me with my students watching in anticipation of the duel. "Go scratch somewhere Dr. Matthews...nobody cares about you...duuuude!" the voices between my ears protested. But I didn't say it out loud because I was a Black woman teaching in the academy and I would have paid a price for my "anger."

Instead, I smiled, nodded, and reassured him that we would keep the noise down. I looked him squarely in the eye, hoping that my disgust was shrouded by my fake Canadian smile. I apologized for the interruption even though I had no control over the manner in which my students entered the room. My smile was forced, hard...and my eyes were glacial. A few nervous chuckles escaped from my students' mouths. I wasn't sure if they were laughing with me, at me, or both. It then dawned on me that the ghost of Shawn, the childhood bully who called me the African Dutchpot was alive, well, and asserting his presence. The academy was simply the new playground, but I felt hunted down in the same way. This time, my man-on-the-moon snowsuit was replaced by a black blazer and like before, I opted for silence, given all of the options available to me. Nothing much had changed.

Stricken with insomnia most nights, I lay awake thinking about the next day's lecture. The workload began to feel more and more physically demanding. During lectures, I drew heavily from my personal experiences and recognized that doing so was too costly, but it was hard to separate what I taught from my experiences. I sensed that my students wanted to learn about me also. After class, a few inquired into my background as they tried to tie the theory that I presented to their own lives. But I found myself holding back when it came to discussions about race for fear of being labelled "biased." I could not afford for my teaching to be deemed a personal vendetta against "innocent" white students. I did my very best to focus on the facts and on "evidence," even though I knew that the evidence itself would be viewed as suspect. I was caught in a racial straightjacket, a racial double bind that I rarely escape as a Black academic.

The fact of the matter remains that my white colleagues rarely understood what I was experiencing. Unless I can engage in serious dialogue with white academics about the extent I am already disadvantaged on the first day of every class, I will always begin teaching from a position of loss. This conversation ought to happen before the start of each academic term, before courses are assigned, and before the tidal wave of the midterm hits. Unless instructors can come to terms with the fact that racialized teaching bodies are often placed at a disadvantage in relation to white ones, the deafening silence surrounding this issue will continue to stifle Black Canadian scholars like me.

AND SO, THAT TERM, as I struggled with episodic depression, I also thought about what it meant to live as a Black woman in Canada. I was born in Canada but I am not sure whether I am truly Canadian. As multicultural as our nation claims to be, I often find myself pleading for acceptance as a "true" and "genuine" Canuck. I am not *seen* as Canadian because I am not white. In Canada, there is a popular cultural story that suggests that slavery did not happen here and because of this, we are not like Americans. Because Africans were enslaved in the United States, Blackness is more expected there, but never here. Despite the fact that wealthy landowners did own slaves in present day Ontario and Quebec, Canada clings to a cultural story that erects our nation as a safe haven for escaped slaves through the Underground Railroad. The story positions Canada as both a geographic and humanitarian lifeline while situating our nation as heroic, virtuous, and without racial stain.

And although life in Canada promised a better life for escaped slaves, Black people experienced extreme racism and exclusion upon their arrival. They were denied land promised to them and public schools were segregated in Ontario. These truths are often left out of our nation's cultural story. The fact remains that Canada has had a troubling relationship with issues of race with various groups including Black people, Indigenous Peoples, Chinese, Japanese and Southeast Asian Canadians. To speak of race in Canada does not ring true for many Canadians because the stories that we tell ourselves about who we are hide a past that we would rather not claim. Issues of race in Canada do take on a different tone than issues of race in the United States because of our distinct histories. The history of Black people in the United States is a history that is well-known globally. The history of Black people in Canada is a lesser-known story.

And yet, Canada *is* my home. I have a birthright to Canada that I treasure, more than I care to admit. After Mami's death, I began thinking more about my Canadian identity as a Black woman living in this country. It's as though Mami's passing made me stop to think about my identity and my place in the world. When I think of that place, I ask myself whether Canada can truly hold me and swaddle me like a warm blanket. It is a difficult question. It is a complex question. Questions about who and what constitutes a "real" Canadian often go unanswered. I struggled with what it means to be Canadian because I am not sure that we have come to terms with it as a nation.

Our national stories shape how we think of ourselves as Canadians. When I think about the national artifacts of our mythmaking, I wonder how symbols such as the Royal Canadian Mounted Police, the maple leaf, and hockey came to mean Canada. How did this happen? When I critically reflect upon how these symbols came to represent Canada, I am instantly reminded of our hosting the Vancouver 2010 Winter Olympic Games. I make reference to Canada's hosting of the 2010 Winter Olympics because the games illustrated the manner we packaged and sold ourselves as a nation on a global stage.

I watched in earnest anticipation, eager to see who we said we were. I was curious to see which symbols would be used to represent something as intangible as our nation's sense of self. The opening ceremony was on February 12, 2010. I cleared my schedule. I could not afford to miss the live broadcast. The first words that were spoken were in French, followed by an English translation. This discursively established the linguistic duality of Canada, right from the start. One of the first scenes that drew me in featured Indigenous dancers and drummers who represented their distinct nations. I watched in awe as the dancers flowed in choreographed harmony. The scene culminated with the erection of three translucent totem poles that stood tall and proud. And while I watched with pride that the games opened with a symbolic representation of Canada's First Peoples, I could not help but wonder about those stories of poverty and suffering that the totem poles hid from view.

In an article for the *Toronto Star*, columnist Linda Diebel (2008) warned that Indigenous youth were discontent and that leaders would be unable to stop their impending protests against what the games represented. Chief Phil Fontaine was charged with being a "sellout" for suggesting that the Olympic Games could bring about much needed reform to Indigenous communities in the area of education, social services, unresolved land claims, and poverty. According to Chief Fontaine, young people did not believe the 2010 Olympics would end poverty and unresolved land claims, offer better schools, safe drinking water on reserves, and "put an end to the terrible situation that causes families to give up their children to state care." Indigenous children are eight times more likely to enter into the Canadian foster-care system than non-Indigenous children, with poverty being the main cause. What was I to make of the fact that these unresolved issues were generally silenced in Canada, even as the world watched the dancers put on the performance of their lives? What was I to make of the dance's hypocrisy? What was I to make of their dance not telling the real story of how they are treated here? The dance hid from view all the social ills that plague Indigenous communities, their cries buried beneath slabs of concrete, muffled and distorted from the fantasy that unravelled on the world stage.

The dance told a story about Canada, a story that was built more on who we said we were, versus who we really are. In choreographed perfection the world saw what Canada wanted it to see. The dance symbolized Canadian myth, a myth of racial and cultural harmony that fails to acknowledge the experiences of marginalized groups in our country. Instead, we are invited to keep our pain to ourselves, to stop complaining. When we talk about being passed up for jobs or about not being hired at all, we are made to feel that we are ungrateful for the opportunities that many of us are afforded as "immigrants."

The entire opening ceremony was several hours in length. I watched in-between breaks to attend to Kennedy. I enjoyed a scene that featured a boy on the Canadian prairies. It reminded me of scenes from Margaret Laurence's *The Stone Angel*. I enjoyed a scene showing a larger than life

Spirit Bear that was lit from the inside. One scene showcased the fish of Canada's Atlantic and Pacific oceans, swimming to and fro through a transparent floor. So much of what the opening ceremonies tried to capture showcased Canada's rich and varied geography from the icy arctic, to the lush greenery of Canada's west and the flatness of the prairies.

I enjoyed the entertainment provided by singers chosen to represent Canada such as k.d. lang, who sang *Hallelujah*. Other singers included Bryan Adams and Nelly Furtado. However, by the time the opening ceremonies ended, Michäelle Jean, Canada's first Black Governor General, stood as the only reflection of me. Flagrantly absent from the opening ceremonies was any reference to a Black presence in Canada. Watching, my excitement waning by the minute, I felt shut out and ignored. Where were the references to my Caribbean culture? Where were the references to a Black presence here? What about Toronto's Caribana Festival which generates millions of dollars for the economy? It was as though Canada was saying to me, "I know you've contributed to the fabric of Canada for eight generations, but at the end of the day, you don't really matter." And just like that my love for Canada turned to hurt and disappointment. I told myself to get over it. I beat myself up for believing that Canada would ever recognize me. I felt awful because I was tricked like this before and for some reason, I thought that this time would be different.

When reading the games as racial text, Black culture did not exist. I wondered if it could be true that Black people had not impacted the nation in any way, reinforcing in my mind once again that although I am in this nation, I am rarely seen. I am told that I, too, can be Canadian, that I, too, can lay claim to this land because my passport says that I am Canadian. Our official multicultural policy tells me that I can be of Trinidadian descent culturally, while also laying claim to Canada, but in reality, it's a much different story.

When the Canadian athletes entered the stadium, I choked back tears of pride, in spite of myself. I watched as they waved to the crowd, exuding youth and exuberance. I wanted them to do well. I wanted them to "bring home the gold," even from where I sat on the margins of Canadian society. After the opening ceremonies, I watched very little of the actual games, except for daily news highlights. When Canada won gold in the ice dance figure skating event, I was overcome with joy. Toward the end of the games when the showdown between Canada and the US men's hockey reached a boiling point, Eric and I tuned in. I choked back tears and forced myself to believe that my feelings for Canada didn't actually matter. I was surprised by just how heavily invested I am in our nation, even as a Black woman who exists on the margins.

Despite knowing that I am not part of the collective national story of Canada, I remain invested in a myth that not only excludes me, but that works to erase my very presence here. When I reflect upon my need to belong to Canada, I recognize that if I do not belong here, I actually belong nowhere. On one of my trips home, Daddy reminded me that I belong to Canada. He said that I was born in Canada and that Canada belongs to me. He said that I should forget about Trinidad because Trinidad does not belong to me. He made it sound so simple. After Mami's passing, I asked myself, if I do not belong to Trinidad, where, in fact, might I find refuge? I remain heavily invested in Canada because it is what I know.

Track 10:

ON THE OTHER SIDE OF JORDAN

Soundtrack:

Tell It Like It Is
Eddie Lovette

Flying Without Wings
Ruben Studdard

Greatest Love of All
Whitney Houston

Wind Beneath My Wings
Bette Midler

Songbird
Eva Cassidy

Sereno Sereno
Daisy Voisin

Dance with My Father
Luther Vandross

Rattle! (Morning & Evening)
Elevation Worship

Not Ready to Make Nice
The Chicks

Daddy passed away on August 31, 2016, three years after Mami's passing. The night before his funeral, I danced like I never danced before. It was the third day of the wake. Friends and family members had visited throughout the day, but the festivities all took place at night. Unlike Mami's wake, which lasted approximately two weeks, Daddy made it clear that he wanted to be buried straight away. Our house was full of guests. The kitchen teemed with women who cooked and prepared the food: pelau, roti, curry chicken, baked goods, pholourie, and chutney.

Near the house, we erected a tent as we did with Mami's funeral, with tables and chairs that provided additional seating. Some of the men played cards. Others chatted. They drank rum, puncheon and scotch "on the rocks" or with Coke. As night marched on, I made my now famous coffee. The heat roared like Dante's inferno and was unbearable, even at night. We did not sleep the night before and watched the sun rise after having a prayer service led by Mr. Das once again. He rocked the house. Trinidad is the only country that I know of where we celebrate the life of the deceased with the exuberance of a real party, Trini style. In true celebration mode, I played the chac chac, while another neighbour beat African drums. We sang hymns and rejoiced in the name of the Lord.

Late into the night, some local boys from Whiteland, all of whom were the sons of Mami and Daddy's friends, began beating the tamboo bamboo, a large bamboo stick that looks like a hollowed sugar cane. The sticks were seven or eight feet high and were beaten into the ground, creating a rhythmic sound. One member of the group used a skinny stick to create a melody while complicating the rhythms and adding dimensions to the melee. From the inside the house, I listened to the beat and was drawn to where they were gathered. Bottles of rum at their feet, they drank using the red plastic cups we use for picnics. The lead singer changed a phrase and the others followed. He led the song with a simple phrase that told a story: "Way Patrick gone, Mama way Patrick gone, Ah say, Way Patrick gone, Mama, Way Patrick gone...," and the others imitated creating a melodious chorus.

I began dancing to the tamboo bamboo in the clearing near the drummers. Compelled by the haunting rhythm, the dance took me back to a time when I danced with the Sankofa Dance and Drum Ensemble in Toronto. The group was community-based and we did not perform for pay. If we were paid for a performance, the proceeds were put towards the purchasing of drums, and traditional headdresses and skirts made from kente cloth imported from Ghana. Although I enjoyed being part of the group, traditional west African dance was physically demanding and difficult to learn. The tamboo bamboo reminded me that I was in Trinidad, far away from my life in Kingston. I danced to honour Daddy. I danced to thank him for the sacrifices he made for me. I danced because he was my dad.

I danced to honour Mami. I wanted to thank her for being my mother, my comforter. I danced because I knew that if I missed the opportunity to dance that night, I could never pay such a tribute to my parents again. At Mami's wake, I wanted to dance to the tamboo bamboo, but I was too shy, too self-conscious, but this time I could not let my pride get in the way. My feet ached after a long day of hosting. Wearing a designer sequined skirt and a beige chiffon scarf, I felt beautiful. I felt beautiful because I could be all that I was born to be without having to apologize for it. Sweat streamed from my brow and ran down the side of my nose. I closed my eyes and danced to the story of how Mami and Daddy saved my life.

TODAY, I AM IN PARABSENTIA. I am without parents. I continue to make sense of Mami's loss at a time when the entire globe is dealing with illness and death. I am happy to be alive given the millions of souls lost to this pandemic. Parabsentia describes a state of grief, disorientation, and mental fog that children experience after the death of a mother or father. Because I could not find a term to accurately describe what I was experiencing immediately after losing Mami, I created it to help me cope.

It brings together the terms "para" meaning parents and "absentia," which means "in the absence of." I am in parabsentia. I am living without parents for the first time in my life. Being in parabsentia has illuminated key truths about my life. One truth is that family is the most important thing in a person's life. Losing Mami forced me to come to terms with questions about my life that had not occurred to me before. With Mami's loss, I became more introspective, more reflective, and more grateful for the life she and Daddy afforded me. When we first lost Mami, I did not think that anything positive would come out of my grief. Instead, her passing helped me to fine-tune my views on motherhood.

Mami's loss also showed me that we must study our mothers. We must study them so that we know their essence. When we study our mothers, we will also understand why they made the decisions that they made, for our sake. We must learn as much as we can about them while they are still alive. We must ask our mothers about their childhoods, who their parents were, and when they first fell in love. We must ask questions about where they went to school, who their teachers were, and which subjects they were good at. We must ask them about life as a newlywed and what it felt like to be a new mother, about friendships, jealousy, sibling rivalry, and about fashions from back in the day. Looking back now, I wish that I had taken the time to learn these things about Mami. I missed an opportunity to really get to know Mami as a woman.

Being in parabsentia has also forced me to come to terms with my purpose on this earth. After losing Mami, I began to ask myself questions about my gifts and how I plan to serve those gifts to the world. Mami's passing illuminated questions about my purpose on the planet and what

I am meant to be doing while I am here. Although I contemplated these questions before, being in parabsentia brought these questions to the fore in new and urgent ways. Rather than swatting the questions from my mind's eye, I spend more time being intentional and strategic, knowing that time is the most valuable gift that I am given each day.

Epilogue

I MISS DADDY. There are days when I still can't believe he is gone. I would give anything to hear his voice again, to hear his laugh and to listen to his scolding. I always loved him. I loved him with all my heart and soul. As a child, I looked up to him and admired him. I remember him driving me to school in his white Mitsubishi. I often stared at him as he drove and I wonder now if he knew. He had high cheekbones and smooth dark skin. When he was alive, I told him that I loved him over and over again. Just before he passed, while he was being cared for at San Fernando General Hospital, he could hardly speak, but through his moans, he kept calling for me. Aunty Juliet would remind him that I was near him and I felt his body relax when I sat beside him and took his hand. And as long as I live, I will always remember how much Daddy wanted me and needed me when it mattered the most. I am grateful that I took the time to visit him that spring. I took Kennedy out of school and we spent three weeks together at the house.

I am in parabsentia and feel alone. I remember now a trip to Toronto that Mami and Daddy took. They were visiting my biological mother and stepfather who lived in Brampton at the time. I was a university student at the University of Toronto and I had visited my biological mother's house, knowing that Mami and Daddy were present. Because I did not want to spend time there, I left after a few hours. Disappointed, Mami said, "Anit, is Mami and Daddy ghul." What she was conveying was, "We've travelled all this way to see you and we don't get to see you often. Instead of spending the night, you are leaving so soon." What I would give to spend that time with them now. I was too busy wanting to go back to James, my boyfriend at the time. I was so young, so foolish. I didn't know then that they would be gone from my life so soon. I remind myself that they got to see Kennedy. They knew that I was married and had the chance to meet Eric. They also knew that I had earned a PhD. I was proud of all of these things. But nothing replaces the emptiness and the void of their loss.

I saw Daddy as he lay in the casket. He looked slightly different from how I remembered him. His face was full. It was as though they blew air into him. He looked smart in his navy blue suit. When I stood near the head of the casket on the night of the viewing, I could smell Habit Rouge, the perfume by Guerlain that the mortician had sprayed to make him smell nice. I gave that perfume to Daddy on my last trip to Trinidad and was pleased that it was put to good use. The casket was a gorgeous mahogany colour with a cream satin interior. Daddy looked regal. I was proud. I was proud that he had lived such a productive life. I was proud that he was the leader of the Jack clan. Most importantly, I was proud to carry his name.

Ten years later, I continue to struggle with Mami's passing. I continue to mourn her loss. These days, I have developed coping strategies to help me get through it. I now use my memory of her as a source of strength, often asking myself what Mami would have thought of an idea or the advice that she would have most likely given me. At Christmas time, when I listen to parang, I try to introduce the music to Kennedy. Each year our tradition is for me to make a lavish breakfast and for me, Eric, and Kennedy to eat while opening presents. It is a special time. I usually play parang while cooking. I try to hold back the tears, but I cannot dissociate the sound of the mandolin from Mami's life. She and Daddy gave our family this gift of music, a gift that we hold on to.

Each year after Mami's passing, I found a reason to go to the grocery store so that I could cry in the car. On Christmases that were too cold to venture outside, I sat in my closet with the door closed and wept. One year I found a spot by the waterfront in Kingston, near Old Front Road, that was soothing and reminded me of her. Even in the winter, I could park my car on the hill and walk to the rocky shore below, in anticipation of the soothing that the crashing waves provided.

Each year, I focus on a new meaning of parang for my family. Sometimes I play the chac chac to a Daisy Voisin CD. I often ask Kennedy to join me. The year after Mami passed, she jumped up and down in pure joy at the sound that I made, even though it paled in comparison to the real thing. I wanted her to feel parang in her bones knowing that once inside, it is virtually impossible to get rid of.

The last time I saw Mami alive was in 2011. For many months immediately after the funeral I struggled to really let her go—until one day, when I received a call from my cousin Stacey. Stacey shared that a friend of hers who had never met Mami before had a dream about her. My cousin relayed that her friend saw Mami dancing the waltz, smiling as she was being twirled on a dance floor. I wept as I listened, grateful for the release the image provided. Content, the sting of Mami's passing began to fade. Instead, my memories of Mami began to occupy space in my mind as thoughts of comfort. I began to rely on my memories of her to help me work through difficult situations. I slowly made peace with being without her physically, even though I always feel that she is close by. Learning of her dance helped me make the transition from grief to acceptance and from tears of sorrow to tears of gratitude that she spent her life loving me.

We must cherish our mothers. We must date our mothers while they are alive. We ought to take the time to create precious moments with our mothers before they slip away. The memories that we create today will ensure that we have precious memories to hold on to in future. We must get to know our mothers. We must ask lots of questions and we need to approach our mothers with the curiosity that we reserve for new friends. If possible, we must record our memories. Today, I wish that I had more videos of Mami speaking, cooking, or spending time with me and my cousins. I wish now that I had kept a diary about her.

What I would give to spend five minutes with Mami now. What I would give for her to see Kennedy growing up. I would do anything for five minutes with her...just to look into her eyes, to see her smile. I would give anything to be held by her. The money that sits in my bank account won't bring her back. The new skills that I am learning at work won't do it. None of my earthly possessions can bring me the comfort that only a mother's love could provide. If Mami were alive today, I would talk to her about my job, my Chanel purse collection, the many dresses that I purchased with her in mind. I would tell her that Kennedy skis, plays hockey and the guitar, and can snowboard. She is also fluent in French. Who would have thought that my daughter could do these things? I would talk to her about my hair and that it is as unruly as it always was. I would tell her about the silly things that rich people buy with their money and about visiting San Diego a few years back. I would tell her how precious Aunty Erroline is to me and would remind her that she used to read to me on the steps of our old house when I was young. I would give anything for five minutes with Mami. Please God, if possible, are you able to arrange for me to have five minutes with her?

Now, when I think of Mami, I no longer see her in the coffin. She stands tall and strong in a white embroidered robe. The robe is long with red cuffs and she oversees the vast open field of my life. She wears thick leather sandals and her waist is tied with a golden sash. She holds a navy blue staff in her hands and uses it to guide her along the uneven path or to lean on when she is weary. Around her neck is a vibrant ruby pendant that sparkles in the daylight. Her silver hair glistens in the sun and her hazel eyes sparkle. She is tanned from the scorching hot sun. Her red lipstick is gone and the natural colour of her lips now shine through. She chops and cuts away the brush or anything that will stand in my way. She breaks spindly trees in half and moves away the heavy logs.

Mami calls out to Daddy. She tells him that I am fine, that I am doing well and not to worry. When he hears the good news, he joins her and they walk together. She sees to it that I am protected. And when she knows that I am down, she sings "Sereno Sereno, Sereno, Sera…" Daddy keeps time as he plays the mandolin, its sound piercing, haunting, and loud. He joins her in the chorus, weaving in and out of the beautiful melody. She makes a way for me. She calls me by my name. And she goes before me, in triumph.

Citations

Chacon, R. (2006). "Making space for those unruly women of color." *The Review of Education, Pedagogy, and Cultural Studies*, 28 (3–4), 381–393.

Diebel, L. (2008). "2010 Olympics face the wrath of young natives, Fontaine warns." *Toronto Star*. Retrieved online https://www.thestar.com/news/canada/2008/05/07/2010_olympics_face_the_wrath_of_young_natives_fontaine_warns.html

Government of Canada, 2023. COVID-19 epidemiology update: Key updates. Retrieved from https://health-infobase.canada.ca/covid-19/#a2

Ingram, A. (2002). What is parang? Retrieved online from https://aingram.web.wesleyan.edu/parangdescription.html

Kobayashi, A. and Peake, L. (2000). "Racism out of place: Thoughts on Whiteness and an antiracist geography in the new millennium." *Annals of the Association of American Geographers*, 90 (2), 392–403.

Moodie-Kablalsingh, S. (1992). *The cocoa panyols of Trinidad: An oral record*. IB Tauris.

Williams, P. (1991). *The alchemy of race and rights: Diary of a law professor*. Cambridge, MA: Harvard University.

World Health Organization, 2023. Coronavirus (COVID-19) dashboard. Retrieved online from https://covid19.who.int

Acknowlegements

To: My Aunty Erroline Lawrence. You read to me when I was a little girl and you continue to feed my soul now that I'm fully grown. You understand and support me in every way and I cannot thank you enough for your care. When I told you about my vision for this book, you encouraged me along the way, and even reminded me about remaining focused to the very end. You are the wind beneath my wings.

I began writing this book immediately after my grandmother's funeral in 2013. This year marks the 10th year of her passing and I can't think of a better way to honour her legacy and to thank her for being a mother to me. There were many who supported me throughout the writing process, which included, at times, writer's block.

First, I would like to thank Luciana Ricciutelli (Rest in Power) for believing in this project. When I emailed Luciana, I was in the midst of my grief and she rightfully pointed out that the manuscript was shaky in those areas where I wrote about Mami. Without her vision, I'm not sure this project would have come to fruition. Luciana was patient with me and understood that I was writing through a difficult time. She encouraged me to work on other parts of the text, until I could write about Mami. I needed that support. Renée Knapp, you did not skip a beat once Luciana passed on and for that I am truly indebted.

I would also like to thank the editors who worked tirelessly on various versions of the manuscript: Ashley Rayner, Alison Isaac, Rebecca Rosenblum, and Alicia Chantal. There were many other professionals at Inanna involved in the creation of this book. Thank you for your support.

To the Jack Family: Thank you for supporting me and inspiring me to bring this project to life and for your support along the way: Judy, Marian, Gemma (Rest in Peace), Juliet, Erroline, Joseph, Glenda, Joslin, Germine, and to my many cousins living in Trinidad, Boston, New York, Canada, and the UK.

To the Davies Family: Over the years, I became inspired to write as I learned more about the works of Canada's beloved author Robertson Davies. At the time, I used his work for inspiration and with the debut of my first memoir, I hold on to those memories.

Dr. Robinson, I promised you that I would send you a copy of this book once completed and you will receive your copy shortly. Thank you!

Maria Lupoi. Bella, where would I be without you. You are so wise and so giving. Thank you for being a friend and a great sounding board for this book and my other projects.

Nuosphere Project. Thank you to musician Robert Nuovo for his work on an original jazz composition for *Lawrencia's Last Parang*. Your creativity is astounding. You were able to capture the spirit of parang and the music of the Caribbean in a way that only you can.

To my colleagues at R/GA and Angie Hannam. Thank you for believing in me and in new beginnings. You made my transition to NYC seamless and your support has never faded. I absolutely love working with you.

Credit: R. Nuovo, Nuosphere Project.

Born in Toronto and raised by her grandmother Lawrencia "Shoon" Jack and grandfather Patrick "PJ" Jack on the Caribbean islands of Trinidad and Tobago, **Dr. Anita Jack-Davies** is a writer and cross-cultural expert. She returned to Canada at the age of twelve and lived in Toronto until graduating from the University of Toronto with an Honours Bachelor of Arts degree in English and Sociology. After obtaining her teaching degree from Western University, the author settled in Kingston, Ontario where she raised a family until 2021 while earning her doctoral degree in urban teacher education from Queen's University. Dr. Jack-Davies is currently Adjunct Assistant Professor in the Department of Geography and Urban Planning in the Faculty of Arts and Science at Queen's University. She works as a Management Consultant: Culture and Operations at R/GA, a global marketing firm located in Manhattan, NYC where she now resides with her family.